PRONUNCIATION EXERCISES
FOR ENGLISH AS A SECOND LANGUAGE

PITT SERIES IN ENGLISH AS A SECOND LANGUAGE

THE ENGLISH LANGUAGE INSTITUTE OF THE UNIVERSITY OF PITTSBURGH

PRONUNCIATION EXERCISES FOR ENGLISH AS A SECOND LANGUAGE

SECOND EDITION

GARY ESAREY

ANN ARBOR

THE UNIVERSITY OF MICHIGAN PRESS

Second edition © the University of Michigan 1996
First published by the University of Michigan Press 1990
Copyright © 1977, University of Pittsburgh Press and the
English Language Institute, University of Pittsburgh
All rights reserved
ISBN 0-472-08376-7
Library of Congress Catalog Card No. 95-61937
Published in the United States of America by
The University of Michigan Press
Manufactured in the United States of America

2005   6   5

Contents

Introduction to the Teacher

This text is designed for intermediate and advanced (TOEFL 450+) students of English as a second or foreign language who already grasp the basic sound system of English but who can benefit from additional practice of the more "difficult" sounds and complex stress and intonation patterns. The segments and patterns were chosen on the basis of an error analysis of the speech of a linguistically heterogeneous group of intermediate and advanced students at the English Language Institute of the University of Pittsburgh.

Procedures for Use

The text is designed for use in conjunction with other materials and is not intended to be a primary classroom text. In the English Language Institute teachers spend from 5–10 minutes per class session on these materials and complete one lesson in about two days. In general all exercises are done with books open.

I.   Recognition and Production

This section has lists of minimal pairs containing the target sounds for the lesson. The students are to listen to the sounds, discriminate among them, and produce them correctly.

A minimal pair drill might be used. The teacher writes the words containing the target sounds on the board and labels them number 1 and number 2. When the teacher says a word containing sound number 1, the students raise one hand. If the teacher says sound number 2, they raise both hands. This technique permits the teacher to *see* quickly if the students have any problem with the distinction. As soon as students can discriminate between sounds, they move to the production stage, repeating the pairs of sounds after the teacher. Directions precede these exercises or are included in the heading. For example, *Repeat,* or *Read and Look Up.* In this latter exercise the student reads the sentence silently, then looks up and says it without referring to the page. Students who have special difficulty with individual sounds can be assigned extra practice with the accompanying audio materials.

II and III.   Stress and Intonation

There are several types of exercises in these sections. The teacher should become familiar with directions for each type. The stress and intonation marks are provided for teacher modeling, which should be practiced aloud before class. Avoid overemphasis. It is important to provide models of normal intonation and stress.

Generalizations and rules precede some exercises. Students do not *always* need the generalization before an exercise, but a brief classroom discussion about language may sometimes be profitable at this level of proficiency.

Many of the exercises in these sections require the students to mark the stress and intonation in their books. Sometimes the teacher provides a model before the students write. At other times, students write without a model. Students may take turns in class producing their answers.

Cumulative Dialogues

The dialogues provide a context for the major points of the lesson and give the students an opportunity to identify the major affective signals in English intonation patterns, such as anger or joy. The same characters recur throughout the dialogues, in a continuing saga of international students making their way at a North American university.

Memorization of the dialogues is not encouraged. The lines are sometimes long and often idiomatic in an effort to convey the flavor of colloquial language.

If the accompanying audiotapes are used, little class time need be spent reading the dialogues. The students listen on their own before class, so that little class time may be devoted to identification and the use of the various stress and intonation patterns.

In many lessons there are questions and exercises that are designed to elicit discussion about content issues in the dialogues as well as characteristics of spoken English. The teacher should point out (or have students identify) characteristics of the phonology, syntax, or lexical items that they hear in the dialogues.

Vocabulary

Students are responsible for looking up unfamiliar vocabulary, both in the exercises and in the dialogues. Little class time should be spent except to clarify idiomatic expressions that may not be found in dictionaries.

Homework

Written exercises are provided at the end of each lesson. They can be turned in and corrected by the teacher or corrected orally in class depending upon the classroom situation.

A Word of Thanks

Finally, I would like to acknowledge my debt to Christina Bratt Paulston for her help in the design and preparation of the original work and Mary Newton Bruder for input and assistance in the first revision. For this second edition I would like to thank Dorolyn Smith and Steven Brown for their helpful suggestions and Lionel Menasche for his patience and encouragement.

The /θ/ Sound

I. Recognition and Production

Repeat.

/θ/	/t/		/θ/	/s/
thank	tank		thick	sick
thin	tin		thought	sought
thick	tick		worth	worse
three	tree		mouth	mouse

/θ/	/t/	/s/
thin	tin	sin
thick	tick	sick
thought	taught	sought
path	pat	pass
tenth	tent	tense

II. Stress and Rhythm

Repeat.

thánks a lót   twó or thrée
wórth a fórtune Míster Smíth
through thíck and thín on the ténth of the mónth

Ópen your moúth please.
Brúsh your teéth twó tímes a day.
Both Tóm and Béth are síck.
Míster Smíth saíd he'd thínk it óver.

Generalization: Rhythm is the alternation of stressed and unstressed syllables. Stressed syllables are louder, more distinct, and easier to hear. Certain kinds of words *tend to be* stressed and other kinds tend to be unstressed.

Stressed Words	*Unstressed Words*
nouns	articles (*a/an, the*)
main verbs	prepositions
adjectives	pronouns
adverbs	conjunctions (*and, or, but*)
demonstratives (*that, this, those, these*)	
negatives (*not*)	

III. Intonation (Falling)

Generalization: At the end of many English sentences the pitch tends to fall sharply. Ordinary statements and Wh-questions (*Who, What, When, Where, Why, How much, How many*, etc.) are usually spoken with falling intonation.

1. Questions and Answers

Repeat.

Question	*Answer*
1. What did you think of the te\st?	I thought it was ea\sy.
2. When did you thank\ him?	Before I le\ft.
3. What's wrong with the cloth?	I think it's too thick.
4. How much is it worth?	It's not worth anything.
5. When did your tooth start to hurt?	Two or three days ago.

2. Interview

Work in pairs. Interview your partner. Ask Wh-questions to gain biographical information.

Example:

S1:   How old are you?   S2:   I'm 24 years old.

S1:   How many brothers and   S2:   I have two brothers and a sister.
        sisters do you have?

S1:   How long have you   S2:   I've been here for six months now.
        been in the USA?

3. Dialogue

Listen to the following dialogue.

Health Insurance

Richard: Excuse me, I need to find out about health insurance.

Clerk: Sure. What would you like to know?

Richard: First of all, how much does it cost?

Clerk: That depends. How many people would be included in the policy?

Richard: Just me and my wife.

Clerk: Have a look through this brochure. It has the prices.

Richard: When would the coverage start?

Clerk: Right away.

Voiced and Voiceless Sounds

I. Recognition and Production

1. The /ð/ Sound

Repeat.

then	this	father
they	that	mother
those	these	bathe
the	brother	breathe

Note: The /ð/ sound is not the same as the /θ/ sound practiced in Lesson 1. The /ð/ sound is voiced. That is, it is produced when the vocal cords are vibrating. The sound in Lesson 1 is voiceless. The vocal cords do not vibrate.

2. Voiced and Voiceless Contrasts

Repeat.

Voiceless /θ/	Voiced /ð/	Voiceless /θ/	Voiced /ð/
ether	either	youth	youths
teeth	teethe	mouth	mouths
wreath	wreathe	bath	bathe

Note: The sounds /z/ and /s/ show a similar contrast. /z/ is voiced and /s/ is voiceless.

/s/	/z/	/s/	/z/
Sue	zoo	lacy	lazy
sewn	zone	place	plays
ceasing	seizing	ice	eyes
racer	razor	bus	buzz

4

II. Stress

Words in Phrases

Repeat.

that's thát   thánks a lót
bóth of them   wórth a fórtune
thén and thére   eíther of them
lázy súmmer dáys   thís, thát and the óther

Fáce the fácts, Smíth.
Clóse your éyes please.
It's a níce pláce to vísit.
Pleáse speák slówly.
Bóth of them are thínking it óver.

III. Intonation

1.   Review of Falling Intonation

Repeat.

Question   *Answer*

1. Who's that?   That's my brother.
2. How often does your mother call?   She calls every other day.
3. How's the weather outside?   It's still snowing.
4. Why didn't she sign the lease?   She says the house is just a mess.

2.   Gathering Information

Work in pairs. Ask questions of your partner. Take turns asking questions. Find out what you have in common.

Examples:

S1: How long have you lived here?   *S2:* I've lived here two months.
S1: What's your major?   *S2:* I'm a chemist.
S1: What kind of visa do you have?   *S2:* Student visa

You might ask questions about these topics:

1. name
2. age
3. address
4. place of birth
5. date of birth
6. marital status
7. hometown
8. home country
9. height and weight
10. shoe size
11. favorite food
12. years of English studied
13. year of high school graduation
14. travel experience
15. distance between here and your country

Rhythm

I. Recognition and Production

The /v/ and /f/ Sounds

Repeat.

/v/	/f/	/v/	/f/	/v/	/f/
van	fan	rival	rifle	save	safe
vat	fat	reviews	refuse	live (adj.)	life
view	few	saver	safer	thieve	thief
vine	fine	invest	infest	believe	belief

Note: The /v/ and /f/ sounds contrast like the consonants in Lesson 2. /v/ is voiced and /f/ is voiceless.

II. Rhythm

1. Words in Phrases

Repeat.

a sáfe invéstment   a pérfect fít
áwfully váluable   a lóvely fáce
a clóse sháve   bítter rívals
a beáutiful víew   fírm beliéfs

Whát a reliéf!
Sáve your breath.
You'd bétter refúse the óffer.
How lóng have you líved here?

2. **Identify**

Listen to the following sentences. Mark the stressed syllables or words.

Example: They refúsed to sígn the leáse.

1. Sing a song.
2. That's a stupid question.
3. You're driving me crazy.

4. They've found an easy answer.
5. Please pass me the toast.
6. How's the weather in Tokyo?

III. Intonation

1. **Review of Falling Intonation**

Repeat.

Question

Who's living there now\?
How fast can you drive\ it?
Why did she refuse the offer?
How often do you visit New York?

Answer

No\body. The place is va\cant.
Only about 40 miles an hou\r.
She said they didn't offer good benefits.
I've only been there once.

Note: If the last word of the sentence is stressed, the intonation falls on the vowel of that word.

Examples:

How fast do you drí\ve?
I don't drí\ve.

If the last word is unstressed, the intonation falls before the unstressed word.

Examples:

How fast do you drive\it?
I don't drive\it.

---

2. **Question and Answer**

Ask your partner.

Examples:

where / good restaurant

S1: Where's a good restaurant in Oakland?
S2: I don't think there is one.

how often / have concerts	*S1:* How often do they have concerts here?
	S2: About once a week.

when / baseball season begin
what / best movie theater in town
where / cheap entertainment
how much / cost to see a movie
where / go for a picnic
when / beginning of the football season
where / see basketball games
where / get tickets for the opera
where / go to get a driver's license
how / rent a car

3. Homework

Ask a native speaker to say the following sentences. Write in the stress marks and intonation lines you hear. Be prepared to say them yourself in class.

Example: She invésted her móney in the sáfest stócks she could fí\nd.

1. She answered our questions quickly.

2. Bev is building a house in the suburbs.

3. Whose books are those on the floor?

4. Whose books are on the floor there?

5. He doesn't save money in the bank.

6. There's not enough interest on it.

7. Phil refused to take my advice.

8. I don't know why I waste my breath talking to him.

9. Which is the nicest house in your neighborhood?

10. Why do you like it?

Rising Intonation

I.   Recognition and Production

The /p/, /b/, and /v/ Sounds

Repeat.

/p/	/b/		/p/	/b/		/p/	/b/
pat	bat		staple	stable		cap	cab
poor	bore		dapple	dabble		rope	robe
pear	bear		soaper	sober		cup	cub

/b/	/v/		/b/	/v/		/b/	/v/
boat	vote		marble	marvel		robe	rove
best	vest		cupboard	covered		curb	curve
ban	van		curbing	curving		swab	suave

/p/	/b/	/v/
rope	robe	rove
swap	swab	suave
pat	bat	vat
pest	best	vest
caps	cabs	calves

II.   Stress

1.   Words in Phrases

Repeat.

lét the búyer bewáre	sáve the bést for lást
pówer to the péople	gíve a vét a jób
báts in your bélfry	a préssing engágement
twélve lóaves of bréad	búy tíckets in advánce

2. Identification

Listen to the following sentences and mark the stressed words.

> *Example:* She néver wéars a bélt.

> 1. Pat's got bats in his belfry.

> 2. People have to beware of bargains.

> 3. He buys pop by the bottle.

> 4. You don't have to have a lot of money.

> 5. Baseball fans never fail to buy tickets well in advance.

3. Identification

Read the following sentences and mark the stressed words. The teacher will not read them aloud until after you have finished.

> *Example:* Léave your pét at hóme.

> 1. Give it to your mother on her birthday.

> 2. The beans are cooking on the stove.

> 3. She was playing basketball and broke her rib.

> 4. Paul covered the bench with a blanket.

> 5. I'll never vote for that bum again!

III. Rising Intonation

Generalization: Rising intonation typically occurs at the end of Yes/No questions, such as:

> Are you go/ing?
> Do you have t/ime?

The answers to such questions usually carry falling intonation:

> Are you go/ing?   Yes, I a\m.
> Do you have t/ime?   Yes, I do\.

Notice that any sentence, phrase, or word may become a question if it has rising intonation:

You're going n/ow?
So s/oon?
R/eally?

1. Repetition

Question   *Answer*

1. Are you feeling any better tod/ay?   No, I'm afraid no\t.
2. You're leaving with/out me?   You can't go\. You've got the flu\.
3. Have you got enough health insurance?   Well, I bought a policy.
4. Are you going to take a vacation?   No, my parents are coming.

2. Recognition

If you hear a *question* (rising intonation), answer, "I don't know."
If you hear a *statement* (falling intonation), answer, "Oh, that's too bad."

T: Is she going with/us?   *S:* I don't know.
He's leaving n/ow?   I don't know.
I'm not feeling\well.   Oh, that's too bad.
It's raining outside.
She's leaving town.
Is today the third of March.
He's not coming today.
The bus drivers are on strike.
Has she left on her vacation.
He got a traffic ticket.
Victor doesn't have a savings account.
They didn't remember to bring their books.

3. Guess the Identity

One student is thinking of another student in the class. Try to guess who he or she is thinking of. Guess the person's identity by asking Yes/No questions. Remember: questions should be answered with only yes or no.

Example:

S1: Is it a woman?   *S2:* Yes.
S3: Does she come from Venezuela?   *S2:* No.

4. Dialogue

Listen to the following dialogue.

At Kim's Place

Kim: Did you get any pop?

Pawel: Huh-uh. I have to go out and get a few things.

Kim: You driving?

Pawel: Yeah.

Kim: Do you have a car, Pawel?

Pawel: No, I use my roommate's.

Kim: Have you got a license?

Pawel: From my country.

Kim: You're taking a chance.

Pawel: I'm a careful driver.

Questions:

1. What lines have rising intonation? Underline them.
2. How do you get a driver's license in this country?

Stress and Intonation

I. Recognition and Production

A. Review of Voiced and Voiceless Sounds

Repeat.

Voiceless	Voiced	Voiceless	Voiced
belief	believe	Sue	zoo
fine	vine	lacy	lazy
ether	either	cap	cab
mouth	mouths	staple	stable

B. More Voiced and Voiceless Sounds

Repeat.

/k/	/g/	/t/	/d/
could	good	two	do
ankle	angle	true	drew
back	bag	wrote	rode

II. Stress

1. Words in Phrases

Repeat.

lét the búyer bewáre	sáve the bést for lást
lázy súmmer dáys	thén and thére
the gíft of gáb	a díme a dózen
crázy like a fóx	dóuble tróuble

You've gót to fáce the fácts.
Thése guys pláy for kéeps.
I néver feel lázy on Fríday.
Thóse two bróthers are dóuble tróuble.

2.   Identification

Listen to the following sentences and mark the stress.

> *Example:* Dón't bóther to búy tíckets in advánce.

    1.   Both brothers resembled their father.

    2.   Very few athletes are professionals.

    3.   They tried two different kinds of juice with breakfast.

    4.   The weather in this place will drive you crazy.

    5.   Two bags of chips are enough for the party.

3.   Identification

Read the following sentences and mark stress. The teacher will not read them aloud until after you have finished.

> *Example:* We tóok a tríp to Bóston in Aúgust.

    1.   Both of the girls got sick at the dance.

    2.   Don't try to hold your breath for more than two minutes.

    3.   The best place to buy clothes is downtown.

    4.   Bus fares were increased by fifty percent.

    5.   She's sick of reading bad reviews of the movies she likes best.

III.   Intonation: Review of Rising and Falling Intonation

Question and Answer Game: How Do You Feel?

One student should think of a one-word answer to a question like "How do you feel?" Other students then ask Yes/No questions to determine the correct answer. Each question should be limited to one word also—made into a question by rising intonation only.

Example:

(How do you feel?)	*S1:* (sleepy)
S2: T/ired?	*S1:* No.
S3: Hungry?	No.

S4: Unhappy?   No.
S5: Broke?   No.
    etc.
    Sleepy?   Yes.

Here are some suggested questions and possible answers.

How do you feel?	sleepy, exhausted, excited, nervous, embarrassed
What kind of person are you?	kind, lazy, intelligent, rich
What's your favorite food?	pizza, curry, hamburgers, ice cream
What are you thinking of?	money, vacation, home, lunch
Where would you like to live?	Beijing, Paris, Saudi Arabia, Seoul

Voiced/Voiceless Changes

I. Voicing Changes the Word

Generalization: Some similar words are distinguished by voicing alone. Voiceless sounds often occur in nouns and adjectives while voiced sounds may occur in verbs.

1. Repetition

Voiceless (adjectives)	*Voiced* (verbs)
close	close
loose	lose
safe	save
loath	loathe

(nouns)	(verbs)
teeth	teethe
strife	strive
belief	believe
proof	prove
excuse	excuse
breath	breathe
grief	grieve
half	halve
sheath	sheathe
mouth	mouth

2. Testing

When you hear the teacher say a word from the above list, tell whether you hear a verb or not.

Example:

T:	loose	*S:*	not a verb
	lose		verb
	prove		verb
	etc.		

3.   **Testing**

When you hear the teacher say a word from the list on p. 17, respond with the contrasting form. Do not look
at the list.

Example:

T:	breath	*S:*	breathe
	believe		belief
	safe		save
	etc.		

4.   **Testing**

Listen to the following sentences. Tell whether the italicized word from the list on p. 17 is a verb or not. Do
not look at the list. Write your answers on a separate sheet of paper.

T:	She was out of *breath.*	*S:*	No.
	You'll *lose* it.		Yes.
	It's a good *excuse.*		No.
	Try to hold your *breath.*		
	Do you *believe* me?		
	Have you got any *proof?*		
	Excuse me please.		
	I can *prove* it.		
	Do you have all your *teeth?*		
	We *saved* a lot of money.		
	Did he *close* the door?		

II.   Stress

1.   **Words in Phrases**

Repeat.

sáfe and sóund	próve it
a sávings account	séeing is belíeving
a bréath of frésh áir	hálf and hálf

Whát a relíef!
You'd bétter belíeve it.
Táke a déep bréath.
Sáve the bést excúse for lást.
You'll lóse your lífe sávings.

2. Identify

Read the following sentences and mark the stress. The teacher will not read them aloud until after you have finished.

Example: Thére's nó excúse for forgétting your appóintment.

1. She never believes a word I say.

2. The dentist said I might lose a tooth.

3. It's safest to keep your money in a savings account.

4. I was relieved when the dentist was done drilling.

5. I could barely open my mouth all day.

III. Intonation

1. Question and Answer Review

Repeat.

Question	*Answer*
Did the pills do any g/ood?	Yeah, they relieved the pain.
When do you have to go back to the doct\or?	I don't have to go back.
Did you ever lose a t/ooth?	No, I've still got them all.

2. Dialogue

Listen to the following dialogue. Circle the questions with rising intonation. Underline the questions with falling intonation.

Kim: What's the matter? You don't look too good.

Richard: I just got back from the dentist.

Kim: Get a filling?

Richard: Huh-uh. Had a tooth pulled.

Kim: What dentist did you go to?

Richard: Just to the clinic. It's cheaper, you know. My insurance doesn't cover dental.

Kim: Well, couldn't they fix the tooth?

Richard: It would have cost a fortune.

Kim: You don't want to lose your teeth.

Richard: Tell me about it.

Word Stress

I. Stress Patterns

1. Initial Stress

Repeat.

> *Note:* Most two-syllable English words are stressed on the first syllable.

téacher	míster	crówded
prétty	Énglish	fránkly
líttle	únder	cléver
wómen	máybe	stóry

2. Stress on Second Syllable

Repeat.

> *Note:* Some two-syllable English words are stressed on the second syllable. If you are unsure of stress on an unfamiliar word, ask a native speaker to say it or check your dictionary.

abóut	colléct	belów
amóng	betwéen	garáge
afráid	enóugh	repéat

3. Compound Nouns

Repeat.

> *Generalization:* A compound noun is an expression made up of two or more words. For example, *girl* and *friend* make up *girlfriend*. In compound nouns one typical pattern is for the **stress to fall on the first part.** The compound noun may sometimes be written as two words, as in *post office.*

clássroom	gírlfriend	bláckboard
bóokstore	phóne call	drúg store
fláshlight	póst office	kéyboard
téxtbook	Whíte House	rúnning shoes

21

4. Compound Noun Contrasted with Adjective + Noun

Repeat.

Note: Stress in compound nouns is different from stress in a phrase consisting of adjective and noun. Both adjective and noun are usually stressed.

Compound Noun	*Adjective + Noun*
clássroom	bíg róom
fláshlight	bríght líght
bóyfriend	óld fríend
Whíte House	whíte hóuse
básketball shoes	néw shóes

5. Two-Syllable Verbs

Repeat.

Generalization: Stress on many two-syllable verbs falls on the last syllable.

belíeve	forgét	admít
accúse	becóme	begín
expláin	recéive	advánce
regárd	decíde	conclúde
suppóse	discúss	reláx
repéat	assúme	redúce

6. Nouns and Verbs

Repeat.

Generalization: Some nouns and verbs are distinguished only by stress. The nouns are stressed on the first syllable; the verbs on the last.

Noun	*Verb*	*Noun*	*Verb*
íncrease	incréase	cóntrast	contrást
pérmit	permít	ímport	impórt
prógress	progréss	ínsult	insúlt
rébel	rebél	cónflict	conflíct
súspect	suspéct	íncline	inclíne

7. Testing

When you hear the teacher say a word, identify whether it is a noun or a verb.

Examples:

T:	íncrease	*S:*	noun
	rebél		verb
	etc.		

8. Testing

When you hear the teacher say a word, respond with the contrasting form of that word.

Examples:

T:	pérmit	*S:*	permít
	contrást		cóntrast
	etc.		

II. Stress Review

1. Words in Phrases and Sentences

Repeat.

hárd to expláin	reláx and enjóy it
belíeve it or nót	únder arrést
a líbrary card	a prótest march

Úse your drívers license for ÍD.
The wórk is progréssing nícely.
The dúplicating machines are impórted.
They páy a spécial ímport-éxport tax.
Tuítion fees are on the íncrease.

2. Identify

Read the following sentences and mark the stress. The teacher will not read them first.

Example: She's inclíned to belíeve us.

　　1. I explained that on the application form.

　　2. The policeman refused to believe her excuse.

3. Kim decided to apply to grad school.

4. The price of the plane ticket was more than he could afford.

5. To get an ID card you have to be a registered student.

III. Intonation

1. Dialogue

Listen to the following dialogue. Circle the sentences or words with rising intonation.

Harriet: Dick, you're going to have to do something about these overdue books.

Richard: Well, you're the librarian, right?

Harriet: A librarian would have you arrested.

Richard: Why don't you return them for me? You could kind of check them in . . .

Harriet: I can't change the records in the data base. I only work there, you know. I need the job,

you know?

Richard: OK, OK, I'll take them back. I'll explain.

Harriet: No, no, no, no, sweetheart, you'll pay. Because unpaid book fines go on your ID card.

And if you don't clear that, you can't register. OK?

2. Compound Nouns

Listen to the dialogue again. Underline the compound nouns and mark their stress.

Unstressed Vowels

I.   Recognition and Production

Generalization: In many words of more than one syllable the unstressed vowel is the /ə/ sound. This is the sound in such words as op<u>e</u>n, stud<u>e</u>nt and sect<u>io</u>n.

1.   The /ə/ Sound

The underlined vowels in the following words are often unstressed /ə/ in normal speech. Repeat.

busin<u>e</u>ss	b<u>e</u>tween	d<u>e</u>velop
b<u>e</u>neath	c<u>o</u>rrect	stat<u>u</u>s
pers<u>o</u>n	occas<u>io</u>nal	<u>a</u>chievem<u>e</u>nt

2.   Identify

Listen to the following sentences. Underline the unstressed vowel letters.

Example: The stud<u>e</u>nts are ab<u>s</u><u>e</u>nt.

1. She broke the vending machine.

2. It's your problem.

3. He didn't care about achieving success.

4. Some patients developed pneumonia.

5. Undergraduates can apply in August.

3. Verb Endings

Repeat.

> *Note:* The endings *-ed*, *-en* and *-ing* are not normally stressed. The ending *-ing* is pronounced /ing/ or, in very informal speech, as /ən/.

spéaking	bróken	repórted
assísted	avóiding	spóken

4. The /ə/ Sound in Stressed Syllables

Repeat.

The underlined vowels are unstressed.

en<u>ó</u>ugh	pr<u>o</u>dúcti<u>o</u>n
fúncti<u>o</u>n	súmm<u>o</u>n
c<u>o</u>ndúct	Lónd<u>o</u>n

5. Nouns and Verbs

> *Generalization:* Some words that change from noun to verb by a change of stress also undergo a change in vowel. In these cases the vowel changes to the /ə/ sound.

The underlined vowels in the verbs are unstressed. Repeat.

Noun	*Verb*
rébel	r<u>e</u>bél
cónflict	c<u>o</u>nflíct
cónduct	c<u>o</u>ndúct
cónvert	c<u>o</u>nvért
prógress	pr<u>o</u>gréss
prótest	pr<u>o</u>tést
récord	r<u>e</u>córd

6.   Testing

The teacher will read words from the list of nouns and verbs on p. 26. When you hear a word, respond with the contrasting form.

Examples:

T: rébel   *S:*   rebél
       recórd   récord
       progréss
       cónvert
       etc.

7.   Identify

Read the following sentences. Find the words from the noun-verb list. Mark them for stress and underline their unstressed syllables. Be prepared to say whether a word is a noun or a verb.

Examples:

They made no prógr<u>e</u>ss. (*Progress* is a noun.)
She r<u>e</u>córded her own voice. (*Recorded* is a verb.)

   1.   We listened to records.

   2.   They joined in a protest march.

   3.   Several army units rebelled against the government.

   4.   The conduct of the troops was terrible.

   5.   Sonia was converted to another point of view.

   6.   Kim had a conflict with another class at ten o'clock.

II.   Stress

1.   Review of Compound Nouns

Repeat.

       clássroom   applicátion form
       kéyboard   téxtbook
       déadline   TÓEFL test
       tést results   grád school

2.   More Compound Nouns

Note: Some compound nouns have stress in each part of the word. If you are unsure how to say an unfamiliar compound noun, ask a native speaker to say it.

Repeat.

cíty tráffic	ápple píe
nátive spéaker	féderal góvernment
stúdent ÍD	párty pólitics
cóllege gráduate	cómpound nóun

Note: This pattern is frequently used for proper nouns.

Repeat.

Mátt Smíth	Pánama Canál
Kím Nguyén	Móunt Rúshmore
Rúben García	Nótre Dáme
Olívia Christópherson	GŔÉ

3.   Identification

Listen to the teacher read the following sentences. Mark the stress.

Example: You have to páy the depártment sécretary to úse the fáx machine.

1.   There's the application form for Matt Smith.

2.   She got a good TOEFL score.

3.   I'm going to major in political science.

4.   My advisor went to grad school at Texas A&M.

5.   She sent a postcard with a picture of Niagara Falls.

III. Dialogue

1.   Listen

Listen to the following dialogue. Mark the stress.

Getting Transcripts

Salim: Is this the line for transcripts?

Richard: Yeah. They're gonna open in a minute, I think. You applying to a school?

Salim: Yes. Grad school.

Richard: Me too. Where are you applying?

Salim: Well, I've got a lot of application forms. I haven't filled them all out yet.

Richard: I hate writing those essays about your career goals. What field are you in?

Salim: Sports medicine.

Richard: Really? I'm going for an MBA. Or maybe law school. Depends on my exam

scores.

2.   Mini Speech

Describe briefly your own experience in completing an application. Be prepared, in a hundred words or less, to speak to the class.

Examples: Applying to a grad school, to an English program, for a student visa, for a job, etc.

More Unstressed Vowels

I. Sounds /v/ and /w/

> *Note:* The /v/ sound is pronounced with the front teeth touching the lower lip. The /w/ sound is pronounced with the lips rounded.

1. Repeat

vine	wine
very	wary
veil	wail
verse	worse
veal	we'll

> *Note:* the following are only near minimal pairs

cover	cower
event	he went
ever	aware
anvil	Anne will
convent	Don went

2. Phrases

Repeat.

fíre at wíll	wórse and wórse
cóvert operátions	a blésséd evént
ívy-cóvered wálls	nó advánce wárning
lét the búyer bewáre	for éver and éver

II. More Unstressed Vowels

1. Review

Repeat.

> *Note:*   the unstressed /ə/ vowels are underlined

<table>
<tr><td>dec<u>i</u>síon</td><td>quést<u>io</u>n</td><td>s<u>u</u>ppóse</td></tr>
<tr><td>admítt<u>e</u>d</td><td>áver<u>a</u>ge</td><td><u>co</u>ncérned</td></tr>
<tr><td>spéc<u>ia</u>l</td><td><u>a</u>ppóintment</td><td><u>a</u>wárd<u>e</u>d</td></tr>
<tr><td><u>a</u>ssíst<u>a</u>nce</td><td><u>a</u>gréed</td><td>permítt<u>e</u>d</td></tr>
</table>

2. Unstressed /ɪ/, /æ/, /ɛ/

> *Note:*   In some syllables with weak stress the vowel is not /ə/. The vowels /ɪ/, /æ/, /ɛ/ may be retained.

Repeat.

/ɪ/	/æ/	/ɛ/
pérm<u>i</u>t	ímp<u>a</u>ct	<u>e</u>nlíst
bás<u>i</u>c	cóntr<u>a</u>st	<u>e</u>ntíre
wrít<u>i</u>ng	ímpl<u>a</u>nt	<u>e</u>xchánge

III. Stress with Negative Auxiliaries

1. *Can* and *Can't*

> *Generalization:* It is often difficult to distinguish between *can* and *can't* in spoken American English. One clue is to listen for stress. The negative *can't* is usually stressed. The affirmative *can* is often not stressed and the vowel may be reduced to /ə/ when it appears with a main verb.
>
>   *Examples:*
>
>   a. Most students <u>can</u> complete the application without help.
>   b. Most students <u>can't</u> complete the application without help.

Repeat.

     1. It can take several hours to complete one application.
     2. It can't take that long.
     3. My advisor says I can't drop the course.
     4. She says I can pass it if I try.
     5. You can apply to several schools.
     6. You can't expect a lot of financial aid.

Identify.

If you hear the word *can*, respond with "affirmative." If you hear the word *can't*, respond with "negative."

1. It can't/can take that long.
2. Some people can/can't understand it.
3. You can/can't fax it to them.
4. Most students can/can't afford applying to several schools.
5. If you get an assistantship, you can/can't relax.

Respond to questions.

If you hear a negative *can't*, respond with "Sorry, I/we can't do it." If you hear an affirmative *can*, respond with "Yes, I/we can."

Example:

T: Can you fill this out here?   *S:* Yes, I can.

1. Can/can't you finish your work here?
2. Can/can't you mail this for me?
3. Can/can't she stay at this school for graduate work?
4. Can/can't they afford this school?
5. Can/can't you guys complete this in a hurry?

2. Other Negatives + Auxiliaries

Generalizaton: Auxiliary verbs tend to be stressed when they appear with a negative.

Repeat.

1. They wóuldn't accept us.
2. The school hásn't received the letter.
3. My application wásn't complete.
4. You shóuldn't expect to get into that place.
5. They áren't offering any money to grad students.

IV. Dialogue

Listen to the dialogue. Underline stressed auxiliaries.

Richard: I've got good news and bad news.

Harriet: Let me hear the bad news first.

Richard: I didn't get accepted by my first choice.

Harriet: OK. Is that all?

Richard: I got accepted by my second choice, but they've rejected my application for a

               fellowship.

Harriet: Why don't you skip this part? What's the good news?

Richard: I can do grad work right here. The department has decided to offer me a full tuition

               waiver, and I'm an alternate for a TA.

LESSON 10

Grammatical Endings

I.   Grammatical Endings

Generalization: The so-called *-s* ending occurs at the end of (1) regular verbs, third-person singular, (2) regular noun plurals, and (3) possessives. The ending has three different pronunciations.

/s/	after voiceless consonant sounds
/z/	after voiced consonants and vowels
/əz/	after /s/, /z/, /ʃ/, /ʒ/, /tʃ/, /ʤ/

1.   Verbs, Third Person Singular

Repeat.

/s/	/z/	/əz/
consists	decides	raises
accepts	believes	chooses
forgets	includes	arranges
attacks	begins	finishes
reports	measures	discusses
presents	goes	catches
hopes	carries	advises
looks	relies	announces

2.   Testing

When you hear the teacher say the infinitive form of the verb, respond with the third person singular.

Examples:

T:	to consist	*S:*	consists
	to accept		accepts
	to choose		chooses
	to attack		
	to begin		
	to measure		
	etc.		

3. **Identify**

Listen to the teacher read the following sentences. Identify whether the verb ends with the /s/, /z/, or /əz/ sound and write in your answer. Be prepared to say in class why the verb takes the ending it does.

Examples:

T:	She *hopes* to go.	S:	___s___	(because it comes after a voiceless consonant)
	He *believes* us.		___z___	(because it comes after a voiced consonant)
	She *catches* cold easily.		___əz___	(because it comes after the /tʃ/ sound)

1. It *looks* like rain.   _____

2. She *finishes* her work early.   _____

3. He *advises* students.   _____

4. It *includes* everything.   _____

5. She *reports* the news each morning.   _____

6. It *rains* every day.   _____

4. **Practice: Read and Look Up**

Read the following sentences to yourself, then look up and say them. Be prepared to say which endings the verbs take.

1. He forgets everything.
2. It just goes to show you.
3. It catches fire easily.
4. She relies on the textbook.
5. It raises the standard of living.
6. She always announces her arrival.

5. **Regular Noun Plurals**

Repeat.

/s/	/z/	/əz/	/s/	/z/	/əz/
events	opinions	buses	pipes	blackboards	exercises
steaks	hotels	lunches	boots	bees	licenses
defeats	stereos	sandwiches	tickets	thousands	garages
strikes	managers	bridges			

6.   **Testing**

When you hear the singular form of the noun, respond with the plural.

Examples:

T: event   *S:*   events
        hotel   hotels
        match   matches
        ticket
        stereo
        lunch
        etc.

7.   **Identify**

Listen to the following sentences. Identify whether the nouns end with the /s/, /z/, or /əz/ sound. Write in your answers. Be prepared to say why the nouns take the endings they do.

Examples:

T: The buses aren't running.   *S:*   __əz__ (because it comes after the /s/ sound)
        The pipes are frozen.   *S:*   __s__   (because it comes after a voiceless consonant)

    1.   The city has a lot of bridges.   _____

    2.   Political events are often surprising.   _____

    3.   Televisions are cheap here.   _____

    4.   My hands are cold.   _____

    5.   The peaches are delicious.   _____

    6.   The pots and pans are in the cupboard.   _____

8.   **Practice: Read and Look Up**

Read the following sentences to yourself, then look up and say them. Be prepared to say what endings the nouns take.

    1.   She eats two slices of toast for breakfast.
    2.   Your opinion carries a lot of weight.
    3.   These stereos aren't for sale.
    4.   We ran out of matches.
    5.   The knives are in the drawer.
    6.   Where do we buy the tickets?

9.   Possessives

Repeat.

/s/	/z/	/əz/
Bette's new car	Ann's new apartment	Liz's new television
Phillip's car	Salim's apartment	George's television
Eric's car	Jose's apartment	Harris's television
the cop's car	the woman's apartment	the boss's television

10.   Practice: Read and Look Up

Read the following sentences to yourself, then look up and say them aloud.

1.   Bette's new car is really nice.
2.   What's Lim's new address?
3.   You can't rely on Liz's husband.
4.   It wasn't the driver's fault.
5.   Lee's mother isn't home.
6.   It was the judge's decision.

11.   Practice

Describe something that belongs to one of your classmates. For example, you might describe someone's hat, shirt, coat, hairstyle, book, bag, earrings, shoes, etc.

Examples:

Jose / bag	Jose's bag is large and colorful.
Kim / earrings	Kim's earrings look like they are made of silver.
Mitch / shoes	Mitch's shoes are good for walking.
etc.	

II.   Stress

1.   Words in Phrases

Repeat.

pláne tickets	kníves and fórks	dírty lóoks
tésts and quízzes	fávorite thíngs	clócks and wátches
úsed cars	líkes and díslikes	hópes and féars

Búy your tíckets at the dóor.
Ríchard pólishes his shóes with óld tóothbrushes.
She réads thóusands of páges a wéek.

2. Identify

Listen to the following sentences and mark the stressed words.

Example: She sélls tíckets at the dóor.

1. He listens to the news every day.

2. Drivers' licenses expire on people's birthdays.

3. She always forgets her books and papers.

4. He relaxes for a few minutes before tests.

5. She meets with her professors every couple of months.

III. Intonation

1. Repeat

Question	*Answer*
1. Whose apartment is thi\s?	It's Lee \'s.
2. Does the price include ut/ilities?	Yes, it includes every\thing.
3. How many roommates does he have?	Just two other guys.
4. Why are these closets locked?	One of Lee's roommates uses them for storage.

2. Question and Answer

Respond to the teacher's question.

Example:

T: What kind of local foods do you like to eat?

S1: Hamburgers are OK.
S2: I only like salads.
S3: Tacos.

3. Question and Answer

Respond to the teacher's questions.

Examples:

T: Whose bag is this?
Whose gloves are these?
etc.

S1: It's Salim's bag.
S2: Those are Carlos's gloves.

4.   Quiz

Read the following sentences and write in the stress marks and intonation lines. The italicized words have -*s* endings. For each one write down whether it has the /s/, /z/, or /əz/ sound. Be prepared to say why it takes the sound it does.

Example:

He *likes* to drink strong, rich coffee.   _____s_____

1.   Buy your *tickets* early.   _____

2.   It *looks* like rain.   _____

3.   She (a) *uses* two (b) *closets* to store her (c) *photographs.*   a _____   b _____   c _____

4.   Richard (a) *cooks* (b) *steaks* as tough as (c) *boots.*   a _____   b _____   c _____

5.   He (a) *carries* (b) *boxes* of (c) *groceries* upstairs.   a _____   b _____   c _____

5.   Homework

Study the following campus advertisement and answer the questions.

Looking for a few (4) good

HOUSEMATES!

3 bdrms (big!) / kitchen / 2 baths
six mos. lease
$200 @ (or $250 if only 4 people)
Carol / tel: 555-3859

1.   Describe the home.
2.   What's big – the bedrooms or the kitchen?
3.   What's the total rent?
4.   Is this for men or women?

Intonation in Compound Sentences

I. Voiced/Voiceless Contrasts (Singular and Plural)

Generalization: In some nouns the change from singular to plural is accompanied by a change in the final sounds from voiceless to voiced.

1. Repeat

Singular (voiceless)	Plural (voiced)	Singular (voiceless)	Plural (voiced)
loaf	loaves	thief	thieves
leaf	leaves	calf	calves
wife	wives	hoof	hooves
knife	knives	half	halves
wreath	wreathes	life	lives

2. Identify

When you hear the teacher say a word, identify whether it is singular or plural.

Examples:

T:	loaf	S:	singular
	wives		plural
	life		singular
	etc.		

3. Test

When you hear the teacher say a word from the above list, respond with the contrasting word.

Examples:

T:	knife	S:	knives
	half		halves
	thieves		thief
	etc.		

II. Stress

1. Words in Phrases

Repeat.

lóaves of bréad   a lóng hálf-life
áutumn léaves   húsbands and wíves
a shárp knífe   hálf and hálf

A cát is suppósed to have níne lives.
You're sháking like a léaf.
It tákes a thíef to cátch a thíef.

2. Identify

Read the following sentences and write in the stress marks. The teacher will not say these sentences until you finish. Be prepared to read them aloud.

Example: They've tríed to sáve móney.

1. She'll have to find better proof.

2. You might enjoy the first half of the movie.

3. Uranium 238 has a very long half-life.

4. Leaves are collected at the roadside.

5. We've done it that way all our lives.

III. Intonation in Compound Sentences

Generalization: When main clauses are joined together with *and, but,* or *or,* both clauses usually take falling intonation. But the intonation of the first clause does not fall as low as that of the final clause, and it may rise slightly.

Examples: I had an appoint‾\ment, but I couldn't go‾\.
             You can go to schoo‾\l, and I can wo‾\rk.

1.   **Repeat**

   1.   Each class takes two hou\rs, and there are two classes a wee\k.

   2.   You can come alo\ng, but you may not like \it.

   3.   Take the application with\ you, and drop it off at the main of\fice.

   4.   You may not be happy with the wag\es, but it's better than no\thing.

   5.   I won't be working ni\ghts, but I have to go in some week\ends.

2.   **Identify**

Write in the intonation lines on the following compound sentences. Your teacher will not say them until after you have finished. Be prepared to say the sentence yourself.

   Example: The salary is goo\d, but it's hard wo\rk.

   1.   It's not what I wanted, but I'll have to take the job.

   2.   I've applied several places, but I haven't got an interview yet.

   3.   I have to work, or I can't pay tuition.

   4.   My alarm didn't go off, and I was late for the interview.

   5.   She has a lot of business experience, but she doesn't have a degree in business.

3.   **Yes/No Questions**

Repeat.

Generalization: When two Yes/No questions are connected by the conjunction *or,* the intonation of the clauses is different. The first clause carries rising intonation, and the second one carries falling intonation.

   1.   Are you go/ing or aren't \you?
   2.   Is she a teach/er or is she a stu\dent?
   3.   Are they going to w/ork or are they going to the li\brary?
   4.   Have they agreed to st/ay or no\t?
   5.   Will she finish the pap/er or ask for an incomple\te?

4. Identify

Write in the intonation lines on the following compound sentences. You will not hear the sentences until you finish. Be prepared to say them aloud.

Example: Are you s/ick or are you going to wo\rk?

1. Did he get a job or is he still looking?

2. Will she have to work or did she get a fellowship?

3. Did she get a fellowship or will she have to work?

4. Have you finished the application or are you still writing?

5. Did you get a loan or will you have to find a job?

5. Dialogue

Listen to the following dialogue. Mark the intonation lines on compound sentences.

Work-Study

Salim: Do you have a scholarship, or do you have to pay your own tuition?

Pawel: I don't have a scholarship. My family has to help me out, but it's not enough. I've got

to get a job.

Salim: You might be able to get work-study. It doesn't pay a lot, but it's better than nothing.

Pawel: Like working in the library, you mean? I only have a student visa.

Salim: I think that's OK.

-*ed* Endings

I.   -*ed* Endings

Generalization: The verb ending -*ed* may be pronounced in three different ways:

/t/   after voiceless consonants (except *t*)
/d/   after vowels and voiced consonants (except *d*)
/əd/   after *t* or *d*

1.   Repeat

/t/	/d/	/əd/
looked	believed	decided
stopped	relied	waited
locked	realized	started
laughed	advised	accepted
priced	agreed	avoided
worked	caused	depended
ceased	happened	ended

Note: The -*ed* ending pronounced /əd/ is always unstressed.

Examples:

decíded
wáited

2.   Identify

Listen to the following sentences, circle the -*ed* endings, and mark whether this ending has the sound /t/, /d/, or /əd/. Be prepared to say why an ending takes the sound it does.

Examples:

We wait(ed) all day.   ___*d*___   (follows voiced consonant)

She look(ed) at the schedule.   ___*t*___   (follows voiceless consonant)

We agreed on a solution.   _d_   (follows vowel)

He accepted the offer.   _əd_   (follows *t*)

1. She stopped taking ESL courses.   _____

2. They relied on money from home.   _____

3. I followed my advisor's advice.   _____

4. He avoided midwest schools.   _____

5. She waited all morning.   _____

3. Identify

Read the following sentences to yourself, circle the *-ed* endings, and mark whether the ending has the sound /t/, /d/, or /əd/.

Examples:

They've never been defeated.   _əd_

She locked the door.   _t_

They stayed all week.   _d_

1. He decided to go back to school next fall.   _____

2. She never stopped trying.   _____

3. They were admitted to graduate school.   _____

4. We refused to take another class.   _____

5. She accepted a fellowship.   _____

6. He hasn't adjusted to the new school.   _____

II.   Stress

1.   Words in Phrases

Repeat.

decíded in advánce	hánded ín on tíme
accépted by Colúmbia	lánded sáfely
ópen énded	deféated by Pénn Státe
repórted in the *Tímes*	inclúded in the príce

They sólved their móney problems.
She avóided taking cálculus.
You're invíted to a párty at the Stúdent Únion.
We chécked the cláss schédule.

2.   Identify

Listen to the following sentences and write in the stress marks.

> *Example:* I expécted to páss the TÓEFL.

1. I'm concerned about getting admitted.

2. She started out in the intermediate level.

3. Kim adjusted quickly to the new schedule.

4. It was reported in the college newspaper.

5. She looked for a part-time job at the university.

6. Richard was disappointed with his grades.

III.   Intonation

1.   Review

Repeat.

Question	*Answer*
1. You mean she got the j/ob?	Yes, but it's only part-ti\me.
2. You mean his grades weren't very g/ood?	No, he had mostly C'\s.
3. You mean she moved off campus?	Yes, but she doesn't like it.
4. You mean they worked in the cafeteria?	No, but they tried to.

2. Dialogue

Listen to the following dialogue. Circle the *-ed* endings.

TOEFL Scores

Salim: It's like I wasted a whole semester here.

Kim: What was your score?

Salim: 520.

Kim: What are you complaining about? That's pretty good.

Salim: I needed over 550.

Ruben: Needed what?

Salim: My TOEFL score. Over 550. Otherwise I paid all that money for nothing.

Ruben: So, go to another school. A lot of schools take 520. Take some courses here for credit.

You can transfer credit, you know. It's not the end of the world.

3. Mini Speech

Prepare brief remarks (no more than two minutes) describing your first semester at school in this country.

Sample remarks:

I was admitted to the English language program.
I lived in a dormitory at first.
I didn't get my first choice.
My parents advised me to come to New York.
etc.

Intonation in Complex Sentences

I. Consonant Clusters

1. Words Ending in Consonant + /s/

Repeat.

looks	beliefs
accepts	hopes
boots	aunts
consists	tests

2. Words Ending in Consonant + /z/

Repeat.

eggs	decides
thousands	begins
brings	bombs
covers	believes

3. Words Ending in Consonant + /t/

Repeat.

pushed	looked
coughed	raced
left	passed
asked	hoped

4. Words Ending in Consonant + /d/

Repeat.

believed	covered
advised	rained
caused	managed
arrived	called

II. Review of *-s* and *-ed* Endings

1. Testing (*-s* Endings)

When you hear the teacher say a word, respond with the *-s* form of that word.

Examples:

                            Verb

T: consist   S: consists
    decide   decides
    raise   raises
    begin
    advise
    catch
    hope
    go
    raise
    rely

                            Noun

T: ticket   S: tickets
    boot   boots
    bridge   bridges
    manager
    sandwich
    thousand
    Kim
    Jose
    Pawel
    Harris
    Harriet

2. Testing (*-ed* Endings)

When you hear the teacher say a word, respond with the *-ed* form of that word.

Examples:

T: look   S: looked
    believe   believed
    wait   waited
    bomb
    rely
    decide

race
laugh
accept
rain
cause

III. Complex Sentences and Intonation

Generalization: A complex sentence is one containing one or more dependent clauses. Both the main clause and dependent clauses take the same intonation pattern as if they were independent sentences.

1.   Complex Sentences

Repeat.

    1. When they arrive‾\tonight they may be pretty ti‾\red.
    2. If you want to buy a‾ ca\r, you have to get a loa‾\n.
    3. We can earn the money ourse‾\lves if we have‾ \to.
    4. He didn't get a fellow‾\ship even though his grades‾ \were good.
    5. You shouldn't waste ti‾\me if you want to get there ear\ly.

2.   Practice

Complete the sentence by supplying a clause.

    Examples:

    a. If you want to buy a car, <u>you should save some money</u>.
    b. When <u>they get their degree</u>, they're going home.

    1. If you look in the newspaper, _____ .

    2. _____ , if you think it's important.

    3. She doesn't have a driver's license because _____ .

    4. _____ , even though he liked the school.

    5. You should go in spite of the fact that _____ .

Note: In complex Yes/No questions each clause carries rising intonation.

Examples:

Do you want to st/ay even if it's bor/ing?
Shall we g/o even though it costs a lot of mon/ey?

In complex Wh-questions each clause carries falling intonation.

Examples:

What shall we do \ when we get \ there?
How can he li \ ve if he doesn't have a jo \ b?

3. Repeat

    1. Do you want to dr/ive if Kim will lend you her c/ar?
    2. Can you r/ent a car if you don't have a credit /card?
    3. Is she going to b/uy it even if they raise the pr/ice?
    4. How can you grad \ uate if you don't take the exa \ m?
    5. Where will you stay \ when you get \ there?

4. Practice

Complete the sentence by supplying a clause.

Examples:

    a. Are you driving to California after <u>Salim buys a car</u>?
    b. What will you do when <u>you get there</u>?
    c. <u>I guess I'll walk</u> if I miss the bus.

1. What _____ if you do well on the TOEFL?

2. I told him I would lend him the money if _____.

3. Do you want me to take the car if _____?

4. How can you find an apartment when _____?

5. If she refuses to listen, _____.

6. Can you be here tomorrow morning even if _____?

7. What time _____ if you leave right now?

8. _____ if you leave early enough.

IV. Dialogue

Buying a Used Car

Ruben: Hey, Dick, where'd you get your car?

Richard: You like it?

Ruben: It's OK.

Richard: I got it from my brother-in-law when he bought a new car.

Pawel: We're trying to get a used car.

Ruben: We don't want to go to a dealer because we don't know them.

Richard: You could try the want ads.

Pawel: Do you know anybody who's got a car they want to sell?

Richard: And there's the bulletin board in the Student Union.

Harriet: I have a car I want to sell.

Richard: You want to get rid of that? I thought you liked your old car.

Harriet: I do, but we should sell both of ours and buy something newer.

Pawel: You have two cars?

Richard: Yeah, but only one of them runs. Hers.

Exercise

Find the complex sentences in the dialogue. Write in their intonation contours.

Falling Intonation and Stress

I. Stress and Intonation

Generalization: In some sentences which take falling intonation, the intonation falls directly on the last syllable of the sentence. This occurs when the final syllable is one which would normally be stressed.

Examples:

Give it to Geo\rge.
She needs time to prepa\re.

1. Repeat

1. Leave it in the gara\ge.
2. We ordered it on the fiftee\nth.
3. The price is too good to be true\.
4. How much does it co\st?
5. I'll let you make the ca\ll.

2. Identify

Listen to the following sentences and write in the intonation lines.

Example: They won't forget to send the bi\ll.

1. What did you forget?

2. He won't tell me the price.

3. Before buying a stereo you should be well informed.

4. They're both nice. I can't decide.

5. I can't pay in advance.

Generalization: In some sentences that take falling intonation, the intonation falls before the last syllable or syllables. Intonation falls after the last stressed syllable of the sentence.

Examples:

There's no warr‾\anty on it.
I faxed them the or‾\der.

3. Repeat

1. How did you find‾\it?
2. How would you like to pay‾\for it?
3. It's a good quality speak‾\er.
4. I found it in the cat‾\alog.
5. When can you ship‾\it?

4. Identify

Listen to the following sentences and write in the intonation lines.

Example: You'll have to send it back‾\to them.

1. When did you call them?

2. Everybody says they're reliable.

3. She got it by mail order.

4. The product was damaged during shipping.

5. I didn't want to give my credit card number on the phone.

5. Identify

Read the following sentences and write in the intonation lines. The teacher will not say the sentences until you have finished.

Examples:

I don't believe‾\it.
Some assembly is requi‾\red.

1. Where's a good place to buy stereo equipment?

2. Leave your name and address. We'll call you later.

3. Salim wanted to send them a check.

4. I thought we should pay by credit card.

5. They don't have a very good selection.

II. Particles and Prepositions

Generalization: Some verbs occur with particles. Some examples are

> look it *up*
> think it *over*
> give it *back*

Note that a particle may appear after an object like the pronoun *it*. Particles are often stressed. When a sentence ends with a particle, intonation tends to fall on the particle (unless the particle follows a stressed noun).

Examples:

> You may have to send it ba\ck.
> What switch did you turn o\ff?
> *but*
> How do you turn the spéak\er off?

1. Repeat

1. Which one did you pick ou\t?
2. If you don't know the model number, look it u\p.
3. We need some time to think it o\ver.
4. Which speaker did you try ou\t?
5. You have to take the cóver \ off.

Generalization: If a sentence ends in a preposition, the preposition is not stressed. Intonation will fall before the preposition. Prepositions occur with verbs, as in

> write *to* her
> think *about* it
> look *at* the price

Examples:

> What kind of deck are you look\ing at?
> You get what you pay\ for.

2.   Repeat

1.   What are you look\ing for?
2.   It's not what we were dream\ing of.
3.   I don't know the name of the place you have to write \ to.
4.   We don't know who we're deal\ing with.
5.   What model did you look \ at?

3.   Identify

Listen to the following sentences. Identify whether they end in a particle or preposition. If the intonation falls on the last word, that word is a particle.

Examples:

T: What are you work\ing on?   S: preposition
      You'll have to look it u\p.   particle

1.   I don't feel like calling them up.
2.   What's the company that you bought it from?
3.   Turn it down.
4.   What kind of music do you listen to?
5.   If it doesn't work, we'll send it back.

4.   Identify

Listen to the following sentences and write in the intonation lines. Be prepared to identify whether the sentence ends in a particle or a preposition.

Examples:

T: What were you thinking \ of?   S: preposition
      Spending money is something I'm good\ at.   preposition
      She asked me to pick it ou\t.   particle

1.   I don't feel like calling them up.

2.   "Amplifier" is the term I was trying to think of.

3.   If it breaks down you'll have to send it back.

4.   We don't understand what you're talking about.

5.   I like a showroom where you can look the stuff over.

5. Dialogue

Listen to the following dialogue. Underline the particles you find. Circle the prepositions that occur with verbs.

Mail Order Stereos

Kim: We found this electronics catalog, and the stuff is sort of what we're looking for.

Luisa: Yeah, since we're staying here for grad school, we want to get something nice to listen to.

Kim: But we can't afford to spend a lot of money on it.

Luisa: Right, that's why we're thinking about mail order.

Harriet: OK. So . . . do you want me to help you out or something?

Kim: Look at this catalog. What do you think about it? Does this look like a good deal? I

mean, what about this ad for a speaker?

LIMITED TIME OFFER!   CALL THIS NUMBER! **1-447-385-9117**

HAVE CREDIT CARD NUMBER READY

RADEX RADEX RADEX (-quality*)
speakers

Were $279.85\\\SLASH\\Now just $184.99/pair

90 days same as cash!!

You pay nothing till June 1st for these features:
- blond oaklike finish
- 4-amp power
- two free 5' cables
- some assembly required
- major credit cards accepted
- call now to receive FREE installation guide

14-day NOOOO HASSSSSLE return policy**
30-day FULL WARRANTY***

*meets *radex* international standards
**from date of shipment
***some restrictions apply

What advice would you give to Kim and Luisa?

Review

I.   Sound Contrasts: Intonation Patterns

1.   Repeat

thank	sank	tank
thin	sin	tin
breathe	breeze	breed
writhe	rise	ride
path	pass	pat
tenth	tense	tent
then	Zen	den
though		dough

ether	either
teeth	teethe
wreath	wreathe

2.   Falling Intonation: Question and Answer

Example:

S1: What's tha‾\t?   *S2:* That's a thermo‾\meter.

Ask your classmate where he/she is from.
Ask how many brothers and sisters he/she has.
Ask how long he/she has been in the United States.
Ask how the weather is in his/her country.
Ask how much his/her (car) insurance costs.
Ask when he/she would like to take a vacation.
Ask why he/she decided to come here to study.

II. Sound Contrasts: Rhythm

1. Repeat

/s/	/z/	/b/	/v/
Sue	zoo	boat	vote
sewn	zone	best	vest
sink	zinc	marble	marvel
lacy	lazy	cupboard	covered
ice	eyes	curb	curve
ceasing	seizing		

2. Repeat

an éasy ánswer	Pléase páss the tóast.
búy the véry bést	You're dríving me crázy.
gét tíckets in advánce	Hów's the wéather in Mississíppi?

3. Identify

Read the sentences and mark the stressed words. Be prepared to say what kind of words are stressed. (See Lesson 3.)

Example: She bóught it to gíve to her móther.

1. The bus drivers are on strike.

2. You'll have to get a driver's license.

3. Don't leave it in your van overnight.

4. I forgot to bring money for cab fare.

5. She slipped on the curb and sprained her ankle.

III. More Sound Contrasts

1. Repeat

Noun	Verb (voiced)	Adjective	Verb (voiced)
belief	believe	close	close
proof	prove	loose	lose
excuse	excuse	safe	save
strife	strive		

Singular	*Plural (voiced)*
life	lives
knife	knives
shelf	shelves
leaf	leaves
loaf	loaves

2.   The -*s* Endings: Verbs (See Lesson 10)

Repeat.

1.   It looks like my textbook.
2.   She reports on the events of the day.
3.   It raises the standard of living.
4.   It rains nearly every day in November.
5.   He relies on his notes.

3.   The -*s* Endings: Nouns

Listen to the following sentences. Identify whether the nouns end with the /s/, /z/, or /əz/ sound. Be prepared to say why the nouns take the endings they do.

Examples:

T: The *buses* aren't running.   *S:*   __əz__   (because it comes after the /s/ sound)
      The *pipes* are frozen.   __s__   (because it comes after a voiceless consonant)

1.   She eats two slices of toast for breakfast.

2.   The knives are in the drawer.

3.   Where did you put the forks?

4.   We ran out of peaches.

5.   The pots and pans are in the cupboard.

4. **The *-ed* Endings: /t/, /d/, and /əd/ (See Lesson 12)**

Repeat.

    1. We solved our money problems.
    2. She missed the first two weeks of class.
    3. He hasn't adjusted to the new school.
    4. I followed my advisor's advice.
    5. We haven't looked at the schedule yet.

5. **The *-ed* Endings**

Read the following sentences to yourself, circle the *-ed* endings, and mark whether the ending has the sound /t/, /d/, or /əd/.

Examples:

They've never been defeat(ed).   _əd_

She stay(ed) all week.   _d_

I work(ed) at home last night.   _t_

    1. I'm concerned about getting admitted.   _____

    2. She avoided taking calculus.   _____

    3. We checked the class schedule.   _____

    4. He looked for a part-time job at the university.   _____

    5. They moved off campus.   _____

6. **Combined *-ed* and *-s* Endings**

Read and look up.

    1. Kim adjusted quickly to her new school.
    2. Classes haven't started yet.
    3. Salim moves into the apartment building next door.
    4. Loan applications are available at the registrar's office.
    5. Richard was disappointed with his last semester's grades.
    6. Rosalia stopped taking ESL courses.

IV. Stress: Yes/No Question Intonation

1. Repeat

Compound Noun	*Adjective + Noun*
clássroom	a bíg róom
bóokstore	a níce stóre
bláckboard	a bláck bóard
gírlfriend	a góod fríend

2. Repeat

Noun	*Verb*
íncrease	incréase
pérmit	permít
súspect	suspéct
ímport	impórt
íncline	inclíne

3. Recognition

If you hear a question (rising intonation), answer, "I don't think so." If you hear a statement (falling intonation), answer, "Oh, really?"

T: Question/Statement	*S: Response*
1. Does she have a learner's permit?	I don't think so.
2. You apply at the State Patrol Office.	Oh, really?
3. You nervous?	I don't think so.
4. Pawel has a driver's license.	
5. Kim won't drive you there.	
6. She got a traffic ticket.	
7. Ruben applied for a student loan.	
8. He works at an auto body shop.	
9. He was offered an internship.	
10. Richard offered to sell his car.	

4. Guessing Game

Guess the hobby of one of your fellow students. Ask only Yes/No questions. The person interviewed should answer with only *yes* or *no*.

Examples:

S1:	Do you practice your hobby indoors?	S2:	Yes.
S3:	Does it cost a lot of money?	S2:	No.
etc.			

V.   Reduced Vowels: Compound and Complex Sentences

1.   Reduced Vowels (See Lesson 8)

Repeat.

> *Note:* Vowels in underlined type are usually unstressed.

profess<u>io</u>n	kitch<u>e</u>n
c<u>o</u>rrect	c<u>e</u>ment
d<u>e</u>vel<u>o</u>p	reduct<u>io</u>n
pers<u>o</u>n	s<u>u</u>pport
stud<u>e</u>nt	pers<u>o</u>n<u>a</u>l

2.   Identify

Listen to the following sentences and mark the unstressed, reduced vowels by underlining.

> *Example:* Some pers<u>o</u>ns are not stud<u>e</u>nts.

1.   The professor hasn't finished correcting the papers.

2.   She's a fairly successful author.

3.   She's been developing textbooks for schoolchildren in Nevada.

4.   Students are sometimes disappointed with grades.

5.   But they were awarded a prize for their essay on secondary education.

3.   Compound Sentences (See Lesson 11)

Write in the intonation lines on the following compound sentences.

> *Example:* It's not what I want‾\ed, but I'll take‾\ it.

1.   The salary is good, but it's hard work.

2.   I've applied several places, and I haven't even got an interview yet.

3.   I have to work, or I can't pay tuition.

4.   My alarm didn't go off, and I was late for the interview.

5.   She has a lot of business experience, but she doesn't have a degree in business.

4.   Practice: Make An Excuse

Suppose someone asks you to do something you don't want to, and you have to make an excuse.

Examples:

T: Have another scoop of ice cream.   S: I'd love to, but I'm trying to watch my weight.
Can you work Saturday morning?   I would, but I have to take my roommate to the
airport.

1. Finish this homework by tomorrow morning.
2. You should get more exercise.
3. Have another cup of coffee?
4. How about another piece of cake?
5. Maybe you could get another part-time job.
6. You'd better make an appointment with your advisor.
7. You have your transcript, right?
8. Can you be here a little early tomorrow?

5.   Complex Sentences (See Lesson 13)

Mark the intonation lines on the following complex sentences.

Examples:

Will you dr/ive if Kim lends you her c/ar?
If you look in the news\paper, check the want \ads.
Why buy a ca\r when you don't even have a li\cense?

1. Will you give me a ride if I'm late?

2. Can we rent a car if we don't have a credit card?

3. How can we get there when there's no bus service?

4. When you have some time, check the want ads.

5. We won't buy it unless the owner gets it fixed.

6.   **Practice: What Would You Do?**

Examples:

T: if it snowed today   S1: What would you do if it snowed today?
                                S2: I'd go skiing.
    if you had a car   S2: What would you do if you had a car?
                                S3: I'd travel this summer.

if you were rich
if your landlord raised the rent
if you were offered a job in (   )
if you could have anything you wanted
if you were accepted by (   )
if you lost your contact lens
if the school raised its tuition
if you found an envelope full of money

LESSON 16

/ɪ/ and /i/

I. /ɪ/ and /i/

Repeat.

/ɪ/	/i/	/ɪ/	/i/
sit	seat	will	we'll
fit	feet	tin	teen
still	steal	his	he's
slip	sleep	it	eat
sick	seek	hit	heat
mill	meal	list	least

II. Stress

1. Repeat

Ápril in Páris	get ríd of it	gíve me a hínt
to éach his ówn	a líttle bit	éasy líving
thrée méals a wéek	a shópping list	hóliday gréetings
an éasterly bréeze	gíve it a kíck	a wínning téam

Can you gíve me a hínt?   Háve a séat by the wíndow.
We éat our méals at hóme.   She's been síck for wéeks.

2. Identify

Listen to the following sentences and write in the stress marks.

Example: I cán't quíte réach it.

1. We'll be leaving in April.

2. Please call in the evening.

3. She's living in Miami.

66

4. He tried to get the window seat but wasn't quick enough.

5. The kids in the back wouldn't sit still.

III. Intonation

1. Read and Look Up

1. Did the bus leave yet?
2. Are you driving to Miami?
3. Would you enjoy driving a bus for a living?
4. You can buy a ticket at the window.
5. If you're driving all the way, give yourself time to sleep.
6. Keep the speed under sixty-five, or you'll get a ticket.
7. You'll get there quicker if you stay on the freeway.
8. What time do you feel like leaving in the morning?

2. Question and Answer

Practice the questions and answers in pairs.

Example:

T: when / leave today	*S1:*	When are you leaving today?
	S2:	We're leaving at six.
where / go last weekend	*S2:*	Where did you go last weekend?
	S3:	We went camping at a state park.

why / go by bus
what / do in (New York)
how much / cost to take the plane to (Orlando)
where / the bus station
how often / travel out of town
where / a place to buy maps
how much / time take to drive to (Santa Monica)
when / arrive in (Minneapolis) if you leave at six

3. Dialogue

Listen to the dialogue. Circle the instances of /ɪ/. Underline the instances of /i/.

Bus Trip

Lee: I went by bus, you know . . . .

Richard: To Miami?

Lee: Yeah. So I'm sitting there by the window, you see . . . .

Richard: Why Miami?

Lee: Job interview. This guy gets on the bus. He's wearing like this prison kind of uniform,

             you know . . . .

Richard: You get the job?

Lee: No. So, of course he's got to take the seat next to me, right?

Richard: Why didn't you get it?

Lee: I don't know! Anyway, he looks like he just escaped from somewhere, you know what

             I mean?

Richard: Miami's kind of hot anyway.

Lee: Do you want to hear this story?

Richard: Sorry.

4.   Bulletin Board

Read the notice. Explain what it means. Where is the person going? Why is the telephone number listed
many times?

```
 HELP!     GET ME BACK TO LONE STAR STATE!

 RIDE needed real bad.
 Will share driving to Austin. April 17th or thereabouts.
 Can pay 1/2 gas, etc.  Non-smoker, not too obnoxious.
 Call Dex from Tex.  After 6 p.m. please.
 _____
 5 5 5 - 4 7 3 8 | 5 5 5 - 4 7 3 8 | 5 5 5 - 4 7 3 8 | 5 5 5 - 4 7 3 8 | 5 5 5 - 4 7 3 8 | 5 5 5 - 4 7 3 8 | 5 5 5 - 4 7 3 8 | 5 5 5 - 4 7 3 8 | 5 5 5 - 4 7 3 8 | 5 5 5 - 4 7 3 8 | 5 5 5 - 4 7 3 8
```

Question Tags (Rising Intonation)

I. Review of Sound Contrasts

1. Repeat

/θ/	/ð/	/s/	/z/
ether	either	sink	zinc
teeth	teethe	Sue	zoo
loath	loathe	racer	razor
thistle	this'll	prices	prizes
mouth	mouth	ice	eyes

/f/	/v/	/v/	/b/
fan	van	van	ban
few	view	vote	boat
fine	vine	curved	curbed
infested	invested	marvel	marble
belief	believe	rove	robe

II. Stress

1. Repeat

fáce the fácts	a sáfe invéstment
thís, thát, and the óther	vóted óut of óffice
ráising kíds	sínk or swím

Lét the búyer bewáre.
She thréw us a cúrve.
The consúmer príce index is on the ríse.
My invéstments háven't páid óff well thís yéar.

2.   Read and Look Up

Be prepared to say which words are stressed.

1.   This page shows an overview of the company.
2.   Let's vote on the proposal after a thorough discussion.
3.   We invested our money in worthless stocks.
4.   The broker charges a substantial fee for small investors like us.
5.   The value fell by 10 percent in one month.
6.   What's the current interest rate on bank certificates?
7.   The manager of the fund escaped with the profits.
8.   A mutual fund may be as risky as the stock market.

III. Question Tags with Rising Intonation

Generalization: A question tag may have rising intonation like other Yes/No questions. With this kind of tag speakers ask for real information but expect the listener to agree. The response usually takes falling intonation.

Example:

You have an accou\nt here, don't / you?   Yes, I d\o.

CAREFUL!
"Yes" means your *response* is affirmative.
"No" means your *response* is negative.

Example:

You're a broker, aren't you?   Yes. (= I am a broker.)
          No. (= I'm not a broker.)

1.   Affirmative Statement / Negative Tag

Repeat.

Question	*Response*
1. You're a bro\ker, aren't / you?	Yes, I a\m.
2. They got the loa\n, didn't / they?	Yes, they di\d.
3. You can borrow the mo\ney, can't / you?	Yes, I ca\n.
4. It's a safe invest\ment, isn't / it?	Yes, it i\s.

2.   Negative Statement /Affirmative Tag

Repeat.

Question	*Response*
1. The value won't go dow\n, will /it?	No, it wo\n't.
2. You didn't sign the agree\ment, did /you?	No, I did\n't.
3. This isn't a con\ game, is /it?	No, it is\n't.
4. My taxes won't go u\p, will /they?	No, they wo\n't.

Note: In section III, parts 1 and 2 above, the listener agreed with the speaker. If listeners *do not agree,* they might add a brief explanation.

Examples:

My taxes won't go up, will they?	*Well, yes, but only a little.*
It's a safe investment, isn't it?	*No, not really. This is high risk.*

3.   Repeat

Question	*Response*
1. My taxes won't go u\p, will /they?	Yes, they wi\ll. (But only a little.)
2. She sells real\ estate, doesn't /she?	No, she does\n't. (She's an investment counselor.)
3. It's a safe investment, isn't it?	No, it isn't. (It's high risk.)
4. These stocks aren't overpriced, are they?	Yes, they are. (Wait a few days.)

4.   Question Tag and Disagreement (Negative Tag)

Examples:

T: you / have an account	*S1:* You have an account\here, don't /you?
	S2: No, I don't. (But I'd like to open one.)
Jose / bought a car	*S2:* Jose bought a ca\r, didn't /he?
	S3: No, he didn't. (He's going to wait.)

you / own a house
(Mohammed) / open a checking account
you / save a lot of money
(Kim) / invest in real estate
you / lose money on the stock market
(Rosalia) / get a car loan
you / advise putting money in high-growth funds

5. Question Tag and Disagreement (Affirmative Tag)

Examples:

T: you / buy bonds

S1: You wouldn't buy bonds now\ would /you?

S2: Actually I wou\ld. (This is a good time.)

you / save money
(Salim) / get a student loan
you / invest in an IRA
(Lee) / put money in bank certificates
you / cash in your certificate
(Kim) / apply for a credit card
you / buy a home here
(Ruben) / open an IRA

6. Explain

Disagree with the speaker. Respond to the question with a brief explanation.

T: Question	*S: Response*
1. You're getting the loan, aren't you?	No, I'm not. I decided not to buy a car.
2. She's not playing the stock market again, is she?	Yes, she is. But she's more cautious this time.
3. It's a safe investment, isn't it?	No, it's not. ( )
4. You're not going to sign the agreement, are you?	
5. Interest rates are going up, aren't they?	
6. They got the loan, didn't they?	
7. My return will keep up with inflation, won't it?	
8. They haven't gone out of business, have they?	

Note: Sometimes, words like *OK, right,* and *all right* are used as question tags and take rising intonation.

Examples:

You're a full time student, right?   (speaker asks for agreement)
Fill out this form, OK?   (polite request)
Sign this agreement before the end of the month, all right?   (polite command)

7.   Dialogue

Listen to the dialogue. Underline the question tags.

Investing Money

Kim: I don't need any of your get-rich-quick schemes.

Pawel: You need money, don't you?

Kim: I need a car loan, that's all.

Pawel: If you had the right investments, you wouldn't need a loan. You could lend yourself the

money, you know what I mean?   And no interest.

Kim: I don't have any investments. I don't have any money.

Pawel: You should.

Kim: I just need a car, OK?

Pawel: Sure. But investments come first.

Kim: I'm an artist. I expect to be poor. Until after I'm dead.

Pawel: That's lunatic. You got your priorities all wrong.

8.   Advertising

You hear the following *recorded* message over your telephone. It describes an investment plan. Be prepared
to explain how much you understand of the message. What risks are involved?

"Hi, my name is William Gillespie, and I would like to introduce you to the Gillespie Global
Development Group Fund.
This is a locally managed, international mutual fund, and we're looking for smart investors.
We offer aggressive, high-growth mutual fund investment opportunities. At least 50 percent of
our portfolio is small, rapidly expanding companies in Asia and Latin America.
This is a 'pure no-load'™ fund.
No '12b-1' fees.
Total operating expenses only 2.07 percent annually.
Just $1,000 initial investment ($500 for IRAs). Additional investments $100 or more.
Keogh plans available.
For more information, call our 800 number now."

LESSON 18

/ɛ/ and /e/

I. Recognition and Production

1. Repeat

/ɛ/	/e/		/ɛ/	/e/
rest	raced		test	taste
edge	age		west	waste
sell	sale		fell	fail
debt	date		bet	bait
get	gate		wet	wait

II. Stress

1. Repeat

Whát a sháme!	táke the tést
sáve your stréngth	fáil the tést
páy the fée	a gáme of chéss
a máke-up test	táke it agáin
a compétitive édge	a pássing gráde

It was a térrible tést.
I'll néver táke it agáin.
She's prépping for the ǴRÉ.
Júst gíve it your bést shót.

2. Identify

Write in the stress marks for the following sentences. Your teacher will not say them until you are finished. Be prepared to read the sentences aloud.

Example: They dón't óffer the tést in Ápril.

1. Let's sign up for the test.

2. You can take some extra lessons.

3.   There won't be time later to prepare.

4.   I'll bet she passes all her exams.

5.   Good students make mistakes too.

III. Intonation

1.   Read and Look Up

Be prepared to identify intonation patterns.

1.   How much do you want to bet she gets a good grade?
2.   What a shame they can't get extra practice.
3.   It's not too late to submit my application, is it?
4.   If I'm not mistaken, the deadline was in December.
5.   The bookstore's having a sale on test preparation books.
6.   How long do you have to wait for them to send out the results?

2.   Asking for Information (Rising Intonation)

Example:

T: find out the cost of a test   *S1:*   How much does it cost to take the GRE?

                                          S2:   I don't remember. Have a look at the application form.

find out if you can take (the GRE) a second time
find out where the test site is
find out when the test is given
find out the cost of sending results to additional schools
find out how to sign up for a test prep course
find out how useful the test prep book is
find out how important the test is to the school you are applying to

3.   Requests for Assistance (Rising Intonation)

Note: Some questions are requests for assistance. That is, you ask someone to help you. These are Yes/No questions with rising intonation.

Examples:
Will you help us prepare for the te/st?
You'll help us, won't /you?

Ask for assistance.

Examples:

T: help to prepare for the test   *S1:* Will you help me prepare for the test?
                                           S2: I'll try.

    explain this sentence   *S2:* Can you explain this, please?
                                           S3: Sure.

help fill out this application
tell where the (GRE) is being given
find a sample test
lend your notes
show how to answer this question
check my work

4.   Dialogue

Listen to the dialogue. Underline the question or questions that are requests for assistance. Be prepared to describe the testing school.

Preparing for the Graduate School Exam

Salim: Is this your first time for the GRE?

Richard: Yeah, I'm getting the shakes.

Salim: Did you prepare?

Richard: I did the practice questions. I bought a book, but I haven't worked through it.

Salim: Have you thought about taking a course, you know, a test prep course? They have

             schools for that kind of thing. I've got this ad. Want to have a look?

Hans Furstenberg's School of Test Success

Improve your test scores by up to 45% by enrolling in a professional examination prep course.
Courses are available for <u>GRE, TOEFL, MCAT, LCAT,</u> etc.
All classes in the evening. All in your community. All at affordable prices: $199.95 for a
complete prep experience.

How do we do it?!!!

In six simple steps. You'll follow the patented Furstenberg™ method, and you will see your
test scores go up dramatically. Make this plan work for you.
Call the local number below, or fill out the application and mail it to the Hans Furstenberg
School in your community.

Richard: I wonder if these things really work.

Salim: My brother took a course. He said it was pretty good.

Richard: Can you make a copy of this for me?

Salim: Sure.

Falling Intonation in Question Tags

I. Review of /ɛ/, /e/ and /ɪ/, /i/

1. Repeat

/ɪ/	/i/		/ɛ/	/e/
sit	seat		tell	tail
fit	feet		test	taste
still	steal		fell	fail
will	we'll		edge	age
it	eat		sell	sale
hit	heat		debt	date
slip	sleep		get	gate
sick	seek		west	waste

2. Recognize

Listen to the following sentences. If the word you hear in the blank has the /ɪ/ sound, say "one"; if it has the /i/ sound, say "two."

Example:

	1	2			
T:	(hit)	(heat)	He tried to ___heat___ it.	*S:*	2

	1	2	
	1	2	
1.	(hit)	(heat)	She tried to _____ it.
2.	(slip)	(sleep)	You'll have to _____ it off.
3.	(will)	(we'll)	I don't know what _____ do.
4.	(His)	(He's)	_____ home.
5.	(it)	(eat)	We forced him to _____ .
6.	(still)	(steal)	I _____ like my brother.

78

If the word you hear has the /ɛ/ sound, say "one"; if it has the /e/ sound, say "two."

	1	2	
1.	(telling)	(tailing)	The police are _____ me.
2.	(test)	(taste)	It depends on what kind of _____ you have.
3.	(fell)	(fail)	I don't want to know if they _____ .
4.	(debts)	(dates)	It's best to forget about old _____ .
5.	(edge)	(age)	The _____ of the table was remarkable.

II. Falling Intonation in Question Tags

Generalization: Falling intonation in a question tag usually indicates that the speaker is not really seeking new information. Rather, the speaker intends for the listener to agree.

Example:

Nice day, is‾\n't it?   Yes, it i‾\s.

1. Affirmative Statement/Negative Tag

Repeat.

Question	*Response*
1. You really like soccer, don‾t\ you?	Yes, I do.
2. Rosalia plays for a team, does‾\n't she?	Yes, she does.
3. The game's on television, is‾\n't it?	Yes, it is.
4. Richard watches a lot of TV, does‾\n't he?	Yes, he does.
5. They've got a lot of equipment, have‾\n't they?	Yes, they have.

2. Negative Statement/Affirmative Tag

Repeat.

Question	*Response*
1. You don't like baseball, do‾\ you?	No, I don't.
2. You haven't been to a professional game yet, have‾\ you?	No, I haven't
3. American football isn't played in your country, is‾\ it?	No, it isn't.
4. They don't play winter sports in Morocco, do‾\ they?	No, they don't.
5. Basketball wasn't played in the winter Olympics, was‾\ it?	No, it wasn't.

Note: A question tag with falling intonation may compel the listener to disagree. When disagreeing, one should give a reason or defend one's actions.

Example:

You didn't get tickets, $\overline{\text{did}}\backslash$ you?   Yes, I did! I went to the ticket office this morning.

---

3. Negative Statement/Affirmative Tag

Disagree.

Examples:

T: (Mohammed) / get the tickets

S1: Mohammed didn't get the tickets, $\overline{\text{did}}\backslash$ he?
S2: Yes, he did! They're right there in front of you.

   you / play soccer

S2: You don't play soccer, $\overline{\text{do}}\backslash$ you?
S3: I do too! I've played it all my life.

(Miguel) / watch ice-skating
you / have a season ticket
(Kim) / has never gone bowling
you / not a soccer fan
(Maria) / go to local football games
you / join a fitness club
(Pawel) / videotape the game
you / run the marathon

4. Affirmative Statement/Negative Tag

Disagree.

Examples:

T: Lee / tired

S1: Lee is pretty tired, $\overline{\text{is}}\backslash$n't she?
S2: No. She hasn't done anything today.

   you / refereed the game

S2: You refereed the game, $\overline{\text{did}}\backslash$n't you?
S3: No. I don't understand the game that well.

(Amir) / can swim fast
you / play for the volleyball team
(Ivan) / tried out for the Olympics
you / were limping after the game
(Carlos) / miss the baseball game
you / take tennis lessons
(Kim) / sign up for intramural basketball
you / forget your racquet

5. Dialogue

Listen to the following dialogue. Underline examples of question tags with falling intonation.

Intramural Basketball Tournament

Richard: OK, you already filled out those forms, didn't you?

Ruben: Well, not quite. Have a look at this one, will you?

Richard: Sure. You know we got our first game at 7:30 A.M. Saturday and our second game at 4:00 P.M.

Ruben: Bring a good book.

Richard: Hey, you're under six feet, right? Our division's for under six feet.

Ruben: What, you mean how tall? I know in meters and centimeters.

Richard: I'll put you down for 5'10".

Ruben: What about this one? I don't get this where it says "Insurance Policy #/Group #".

Richard: That's health insurance.

Ruben: I know mine's something like Mutual or State Life . . . I don't know the numbers.

Richard: I'll put you down the same as mine.

Ruben: And this one. What does that mean?

   ". . . and I hereby waive all legal rights to claims for damages resulting from personal injury or accidental death and absolve the athletic department and the university from all responsibility for said injury or accident consequent to my participation in this event. . . ."

Richard: That's so you can't sue them. If you get hurt, you're not going to sue them, are you?

Ruben: Well, I might want to.

Richard: Never mind. Sign it. We're in.

Additional Questions

1. What is meant by the expression **5'10"** ?
2. What does the symbol # mean in this dialogue?
3. Explain what is meant by the phrase "**claims for damages**"?

/ʊ/ and /u/

I.   /ʊ/   and   /u/

Repeat.

/ʊ/	/u/
could	cooed
would	wooed
should	shoed
look	Luke
full	fool
pull	pool

II.   Stress

1.   Repeat

a góod cóokbook	a cóoking school
júice and cóffee	spóon and fórk
cóokies and mílk	a góod móod
the cúlinary art	the kítchen nóok

Tóo many cóoks spóil the bróth.
She púlled the wóol over your éyes.
Táke a lóok at the fóod.
Whó tóok my spóon?

2.   Read and Look Up

Be prepared to identify stressed syllables.

1. Want to buy a ticket to the international student dinner?
2. What have you got to lose?
3. We're putting on a little play.
4. I have to follow the recipe in the cookbook.
5. She's a graduate of a culinary school.
6. You have to help out with the cooking.
7. I'd rather do the cleaning up.
8. Who's footing the bill?

III. Intonation

1. Review of Question Tags

Repeat.

Question	*Response*
1. You're a good cook, are‾\n't you?	So-so.
2. You didn't say anything rude to the host, did̲ /you?	No, but I should have!
3. He refused to buy a ticket, r/ight?	No, he bought two.
4. I'm looking at your cookbook, O/ K?	Sure.
5. They put something in the rice, did̲/n't they?	Looks funny to me.

2. Polite Requests

Suppose you are organizing an international student dinner.

> *Note:* Polite requests often end with rising intonation. Remember that if you refuse a request, you should explain *why* you have to refuse.

Examples:

T: speak at the international student dinner

S1: Could you please give a short speech at our dinner next Wednesday evening?

S2: I'd love to, but I'm going to be out of town next week.

buy a ticket to the international student dinner
help us organize the dinner
help out with the cooking
be willing to work in the kitchen
sell tickets for us
announce this to your class
drive us to the store
lend me your car
inquire about renting the hall
buy advertising in our program
proofread our advertising flyer
help set up the tables and clean up afterward
tell me how to get to the auditorium where they're having the international student dinner
explain how you prepared this (beriyani chicken)

3. **Dialogue**

Somebody's Got to Do It . . .

Salim:	I know I said I would help. But I don't know . . . .
Richard:	This looks pretty hard.
Kim:	Well, I don't have anybody else who can do it. Just do the best you can, will you? There's not much time left. Besides, you can't wreck peanut sauce. Just follow the instructions on the card.

Ingredients

2 tbsp oil

310 g (10 oz) fried peanuts – skinned and chopped or processed in blender/food
*   processor into chunky bits (or, if desperate, substitute chunky peanut butter)*

1/4 tsp shrimp paste

2 or 3 red chilis — seeded and chopped

2 cloves garlic — chopped

3 tsp brown sugar

1 tbsp lime juice

1-3/4 cups coconut milk (available in cans)

salt to taste

Salim:	Where are we supposed to get all this?
Richard:	Some of it I've got at home. I guess we'll have to run to the supermarket for the rest. Why do you have to put shrimp in peanut butter, I wonder. Yuck.
Salim:	Do you really know how to cook?
Richard:	I can do spaghetti and stuff.
Salim:	What's *tsp?*
Richard:	That's a spoonful.
Salim:	Then what's *tbsp?*
Richard:	A spoon, I guess. Maybe it's a typo.
Salim:	So, what are we supposed to do with all these things?
Richard:	We'll just mix it in a bowl and put it in the oven. She said we couldn't wreck it. It'll be okay. I've cooked before.

Questions

1. What's a *tbsp?* A *typo?*
2. How many grams in an ounce?
3. What is missing from the recipe above? (See the next page.)

Richard and Salim forgot to look at the other side of the recipe card on which the instructions were printed.

Instructions

To prepare sauce:
1. *Heat oil in large saucepan. Fry all sauce ingredients, except coconut milk, on medium heat for five minutes, stirring constantly.*
2. *Reduce heat and add coconut milk. Let simmer uncovered until sauce thickens, stirring often.*
3. *Remove from heat.*
4. *Can be poured over vegetables or used as dip.*

---

4.   Practical Exercise

Explain the instructions in your own words. Try the recipe. Share with classmates.

Falling Intonation in Special Emphasis

I. Listen

Rosalia: I _have_ to drive there this weekend. My aunt wants her car back.

Pawel: I wish _I_ had an aunt who'd lend me her car.

Generalization: Falling intonation and stress usually come together at the end of a sentence. Sometimes, to give a word strong emphasis or to clarify the meaning, the word is heavily stressed. Intonation may also fall at that point.

Example:

She has to drive her aunt's car to De$\overline{}$\nver. (normal pattern)

a. Special emphasis on <u>aunt</u>
    She has to drive her *áunt's*\ car to Denver. (not her uncle's)
b. Special emphasis on <u>has to</u>
    She *hás*\ *to* drive her aunt's car to Denver. (She has no choice.)
c. Special emphasis on <u>she</u>
    Shé\ has to drive her aunt's car to Denver. (she, not someone else)

---

2. Repeat

1. He's driving his uncle's car to San Die\go.
2. He's driving his uncle's \car to San Diego.
3. He's driv\ing his uncle's car to San Diego.
4. He'\s driving his uncle's car to San Diego.

3. Practice

Listen to the following sentences. Say each sentence applying special emphasis to the cue word.

1. They planned to take the bus to Detroi\t.

T:	bus	*S1:*	They planned to take the *bus*\ to Detroit.
	planned	*S2:*	They *planned*\ to take the bus to Detroit.
	they	*S3:*	

2. I'm thinking about flying home during the brea\k.
   T: home   S1:
        flying
        thinking

3. We're renting a car to go camping this sum\mer.
   T: this
        camping
        car
        renting

4. You have to take the turnpike east for eleven mi\les.
   T: east
        turnpike
        have

II.   Special Emphasis with Question Tags

1.   Practice

Listen to the following sentences. Apply special emphasis to the cue words. When you answer questions, deny the point that is emphasized.

1. You didn't buy a used car from Smalley's, did／you?
   T: car   S1: You didn't buy a used *ca\r* from Smalley's, did／you?
                       S2: No. I bought a van.
        used   S2: You didn't buy a *used* \car from Smalley's, did／you?
                       S3: No. I bought a new car.
        buy   S3: You didn't *buy* \a used car from Smalley's, did／you?
                       S4: No. I leased it.

2. You don't have to drive there this weekend, do／you?
   T: this
        there
        drive
        have to

3. Rosalia didn't ask to borrow her aunt's car for the trip, did／she?
   T: car
        aunt's
        ask

4. Pawel doesn't have an uncle in Chicago, does／he?
   T: uncle
        Pawel

5. They agreed to pay half the car insurance, didn't/they?
    T: half
             agreed

6. You don't pay the insurance on your brother's old car, do/you?
    T: old
             brother's

III. Special Emphasis and Contrast

Note: Sometimes special emphasis may help clarify the meaning of the speaker or to contrast two ideas.

Example:

I *drove* all the way. You just *sat* there.

1. Repeat

1. I wouldn't *buy* a new van; I might *lease* one.
2. *You* go pick him up. He's *your* uncle after all.
3. There's a *left* exit and a *right* exit. You take the *left* exit.
4. *I* didn't leave the keys in there. *You* did.

2. Practice

Use the paired words in a sentence or sentences with strong emphasis.

Example:

T: rent / lease   *S:* I didn't say *lease* the car. I said I was *renting* a car.

you / I
left / right
new / used
uncle / aunt
turnpike / freeway
drive to Detroit / fly to Detroit
under the speed limit / over

IV. Dialogue

Listen to the dialogue. Circle instances of special emphasis.

Rosalia: I have to drive there this weekend. My aunt wants her car back.

Kim: I thought it was your car.

Rosalia: No, I was just using it.

Pawel: I wish I had an aunt who'd lend me her car. I wish I had an aunt who had a car.

Kim: I thought your aunt lived around here.

Rosalia: No, I have my . . . uh . . . other aunt's car. The one from San Jose.

Pawel: How many cars does she have?

Rosalia: No, I have two aunts, okay? And one car they have.

Pawel: They share it?

Rosalia: No!

Kim: Just ignore him. He's jealous.

LESSON 22

/l/ and /r/

I. Recognizing the Sounds

1. Repeat

/l/	/r/	/l/	/r/	/l/	/r/
late	rate	cloud	crowd	tile	tire
law	raw	flee	free	role	roar
lead	read	rolling	roaring	stole	store
lice	rice	miller	mirror	coal	core
light	right	glass	grass	steal	steer
lock	rock	collect	correct	dial	dire
low	row	files	fires	file	fire
long	wrong	believed	bereaved	wall	war

2. Identify

Listen to the following sentences. If the word in the blank has the /l/ sound, say "one"; if it has the /r/ sound, say "two."

Example:

	1	2		
T:	(lock)	(rock)	We couldn't break the ___rock___ .	*S:* 2

	1	2		
1.	(lock)	(rock)	She broke the _____ .	*S:*
2.	(long)	(wrong)	They gave us the _____ one.	
3.	(flee)	(free)	The Colonel refused to _____ the city.	
4.	(cloud)	(crowd)	It disappeared into the _____ .	

5. (glass)   (grass)   You can't walk barefoot on the _____ .

6. (Collect) (Correct) _____ the papers, please.

7. (file)   (fire)   The papers were lost in the _____ .

II. Stress

1. Repeat

lóts of lúck	crówd control
róck 'n róll	fréezing cóld
a stólen cár	létters to the éditor
ríght and wróng	fórest fires
rhýthm 'n blúes	láw and órder

Colléct the pápers.
Évery clóud has a sílver líning.
Túrn your pápers in tomórrow.
Háve your éditor lóok it óver first.

2. Read and Look Up

Be prepared to identify stressed syllables.

1. Julio was tired after writing the paper.
2. He was so tired he fell asleep during the final exam.
3. During the semester break Julio rested for a few days.
4. He met his friends at the mall one Saturday.
5. Julio looked in the technology store for new software.
6. Salim was looking for a new word processor that had a good spell check.
7. They finally found a product with an excellent grammar check too.
8. When classes resumed, they felt they'd be ready.
9. This semester they would be taking at least one class for college credit.
10. Julio was a little nervous about writing research papers in English.

III. Intonation

1.   Review of Tag Questions

Repeat.

	Question	*Answer*
1.	We go ri\ght here, don't /we?	No, le\ft.
2.	We turn right he\re, don't /we?	No, at the end of the ha\ll.
3.	This is the wri\ting center, isn't /it?	This is i\t.
4.	There's no cha\rge for this, r/ight?	Ri\ght. It's free\.
5.	I need some gra\mmar help, O/K?	Let's have a loo\k.

2.   Misunderstandings

Read the sentences to yourself. Select one of the words in parentheses. Then look up and say the sentence aloud.

When your teacher asks a question, repeat the sentence giving special emphasis to the word you have selected.

Example:

S1:   I don't want to be the one who (*collects, corrects*) the papers.
T: Did you say *collects* or *corrects?*
S1:   I don't want to *corre\ct* the papers.

1. It's not my job to (*collect, correct*) the papers.
2. We walked into the (*long, wrong*) hallway.
3. Make sure you pick up the (*light, right*) package.
4. When you're done with the paper, toss it in the (*file, fire*).
5. What a vacation. I had a terrible (*flight, fright*).
6. Look it up under (*miller, mirror*) in the dictionary.
7. (*Collecting, correcting*) the tests wasn't that hard a job.
8. I was waiting in the (*long, wrong*) line.
9. There was cut (*glass, grass*) on the floor.
10. How come I never get the (*light, right*) job?

3. Dialogue

Listen to the dialogue. Write the correct word in the space provided.

Using the Writing Center

Kim: This is my first real paper. I mean, for a _____ course.

Salim: You're a good _____ . It'll be OK.

Kim: I was OK in ESL, but this is _____ for real.

Salim: Have somebody take a _____ at it.

Kim: I don't know anybody, _____. My roommates are _____ from Korea.
They're no better than me.

Salim: Try the Writing Center. They have _____ .

Kim: _____ they any good? Maybe I'll just go to the computer center and use

their _____. Do they have a grammar check?

Salim: It's no good. It accepts my papers even when they're _____ . Get a tutor.

Kim: OK. I'll try the Writing _____ then. Where is it anyway?

4. Critique Yourself

Describe briefly what you do well and what you do poorly in writing English. What are your problem
areas? What's harder (or easier) about writing in English compared with your first language?

Rising Intonation in Special Emphasis

I.   Introduction

Generalization: Yes/No question intonation usually rises on the last stressed syllable at the end of the sentence. But if the speaker places special emphasis on a word earlier in the sentence, the intonation may rise at that point. (See Lesson 21 for Falling Intonation in Special Emphasis.)

Example:

Did Dick buy Harriet a Spanish dictionary for her birth/day? (normal intonation)

   a.   Special emphasis on *Spanish*
      Did Dick buy Harriet a *Sp/anish* dictionary for her birthday? (not a Japanese dictionary)
   b.   Special emphasis on *Harriet*
      Did Dick buy *H/arriet* a Spanish dictionary for her birthday? (not Kim)
   c.   Special emphasis on *Dick*
      Did *D/ick* buy Harriet a Spanish dictionary for her birthday? (not Julio)

1.   Repetition

1.   What are you doing this weekend?
2.   Are you going to wash your car *Satu/rday*?
3.   Are you going to *w/ash* your car Saturday?
4.   Are *y/ou* going to wash your car Saturday?
5.   Do you already have tickets for Friday night's *con/cert*?
6.   Do you already have tickets for *Fri/day* night's concert?
7.   Do you *al/ready* have tickets for Friday night's concert?

2.   Practice

Listen and repeat the sentence. Then say the sentence again applying special emphasis to the cue word.

   1.   Are you taking the bus to Las Vegas this *w/eekend*?

T:	Las Vegas	*S1:*	Are you taking the bus to *Las V/egas* this weekend?
T:	bus	*S2:*	Are you taking the *b/us* to Las Vegas this weekend?
T:	you	*S3:*	Are *y/ou* taking the bus to Las Vegas this weekend?

2. Do you already have tickets for Friday night's game?
   T: Friday
        already
        you

3. Do you have to go to the laundromat this weekend?
   T: this
        laundromat
        have to

4. Would you like to have lunch with us at the mall Saturday?
   T: mall
        us
        lunch

5. Do you still want to study in the library all weekend?
   T: all
        library
        still

II. Intonation

1. Respond to Special Emphasis

Listen and repeat the sentence. Apply special emphasis to make a question. When you answer such a question, deny the point that is emphasized.

1. Are you going to wash your car Sunday _m/orning_?

T:	Sunday	*S1:*	Are you going to wash your car _S/unday_ morning?
		S2:	No. I'm going to wash it tomorrow.
T:	car	*S2:*	Are you going to wash your _c/ar_ Sunday morning?
		S3:	No. I'm going to wash clothes.
T:	your	*S3:*	Are you going to wash _y/our_ car Sunday morning?
		S4:	No. I have to wash Pawel's car.

2. Did your aunt promise to lend you her car for the weekend?
   T: car
        promise
        aunt

3. Are you really going to spend the whole weekend with your aunt?
   T: weekend
        really

4. Are you sure we have to have this paper done by Monday?
   T: done
        have to
        sure

5. Can we finish this paper before Friday afternoon?
   T: before
        finish

2. Double Emphasis

Note: Speakers may place special emphasis on two items in a Yes/No question to indicate surprise. In this case, intonation rises on each item that receives special emphasis.

Examples:

He mixes l/emons with the p/eanuts?
Do you put /onions in your s /oup?

Repeat.

1. Does she mix l/emons with the p/eanuts?
2. Do they put /onions in their s /oup?
3. You put p/epper in your /eggs?
4. Did they put h /ot sauce in their n /oodles?
5. Did they mix jalap/eño in this s /alad?
6. Does she put m/int in her p/izza sauce?
7. Did you put guacam/ole on the v /egetables?
8. Did somebody put c/innamon in my espr/esso?

3. Respond

Make a question with double emphasis using the pairs of words that follow. Respond to the question with an explanation.

Example:

T: onions / soup	*S1:* Do you put /onions in your s /oup?
	S2: Sure. It's French.

pepper / eggs
tumeric / rice
guacamole / salad
soy sauce / stir fry
vanilla / latte
hot sauce / chow mein
jalapeño / pizza
avocado / sandwich

4.   Polite Suggestions

You want to suggest to Ruben that he get some of his school work done this weekend. Make these suggestions by using questions. By answering "no," Ruben declines to follow your suggestion.

Example:

S1:   Don't you have a test to study for?
Ruben: No. I think I already know the material OK.
S2:   Aren't you supposed to finish your paper this weekend?
Ruben: No. There's no hurry. I still have a week to finish it.

Don't you have a paper to write for Monday?
Aren't you supposed to give an oral report next week?
Haven't you got an assignment due Monday?
Don't you think you've watched enough basketball this weekend?
Have you forgotten about that little test that you're going to have Monday morning?
Didn't your grades go down a little last semester?
Don't you think it's about time you got to work on that paper?
Do you really know the material in this chapter?
Would you like some help?

III.   Dialogue

Listen to the dialogue. Circle the questions which you think are suggestions that Ruben should go to the game.

The Playoffs

Ruben: You got what to go where?

Richard: You heard me. Four tickets to the playoffs in Philadelphia.

Ruben: This weekend?

Richard: Yup. Wanna go?

Ruben: I don't know. My friends from last semester are having this dinner.

Richard: I'd stay away from dinners. Remember the last one? That peanut sauce?

Ruben: I remember. But I'm not cooking. Also, you know, I've got a lot of school work this

         weekend.

Richard: Don't you think you're taking things a little too serious? I mean, homework? It's not

            like finals are coming up or anything.

Ruben: It's due Monday.

Richard: Can't you like take it with you? Do it at the game, maybe?

Ruben: I have to write a paper.

Richard: Well, bring a laptop.

Ruben: Yeah, I guess I could.

LESSON 24

/l/ and /r/ Clusters

I. /l/ and /r/

1. Repeat

blend	called	health
glass	filled	shelf
class	built	film
plate	silk	involve
climb	milk	help

drive	broken	quart	horse
drink	breeze	burn	first
practice	throw	girl	cars
traffic	scratch	born	worst
thrill	scream	learn	world

II. Stress

1. Repeat

tráffic accident	fénder bender
drúnk dríver	désignated dríver
séatbelt	emérgency room
lícense plates	cár insurance

Pléase fásten your séatbelts.
Dón't drínk and dríve.
She was thrówn from the cár.
Did ánybody stóp to hélp?

2. Read and Look Up

1. The drive down the coast was very pleasant.
2. The northbound freeway has the worst rush hour traffic.
3. It was hard learning how to drive on city streets.
4. I'm not sure if learning to drive is worth the effort.
5. She crashed into the guard rail on the bridge.

6. She got scratched by some broken glass.
7. Car insurance will take care of the collision damage.
8. Most of the hospital bills should be covered under health insurance.

III. Intonation: Series/Surprise

> *Generalization:* Items in a series often take rising intonation. The last item in a series making up a sentence will usually take falling intonation.
>
> *Examples:*
>
> We w/ashed the car, w/axed it, cl/eaned out the inside, and then drove it downtow\n.
> I stopped to order a h/amburger, an order of fr/ies, a cup of c/offee and a sa\lad.

1. Repeat

1. I had to pay the r/ental, a m/ileage fee, two kinds of ins/urance, and of course I have to pay for ga\s.
2. We had a flat t/ire, ran out of g/as, lost our tr/aveler's checks, and then got lo\st.
3. First I had to pick up the t/ickets, get something for d/inner, drop off l/ibrary books, and then get cha\nged.
4. I turned into a one-way street the wrong w/ay, then back\ed/ out, then turned into 4th Str/eet when I should have taken 4th Ave. SW, then I made a U-t/urn and got onto the freeway by mista\ke.

2. Read and Look Up

1. We washed the car, waxed it, vacuumed the inside, and then drove downtown.
2. I stopped to order a hamburger, an order of fries, a cup of coffee, and a salad.
3. I picked up Kim, and we went to the supermarket, then I had to get gas, then I had to stop at an ATM because I used up all my cash, then finally we headed for home.
4. I looked both ways, I pulled out slowly, I had my signal on, I had my lights on, I did everything right!

> *Generalization:* Question words (*who, what,* etc.) are sometimes spoken with rising intonation. In this case the speaker is not really asking for new information. The question word is really an expression of surprise or disbelief or misunderstanding.
>
> *Examples:*
>
> Rosalia had a traffic accident.　　　　　Wh/at?
> She was out on the freeway.　　　　　　Wh/ere?

3. Repeat

Listen to the sentence. Repeat the question word.

1. She may have to quit school.   Wh/at?
2. She's in the hospital.   Wh/ere?
3. She may not get out till next month. Wh/en?

4. Practice

Examples:

T: have an accident / what   *S1:* Ernesto had a little accident.
                                       S2: Wh/at?
                                       S1: He's OK. He just had a little fender bender.

T: professor wrecked his car / who   *S2:* My physics prof wrecked his car.
                                       S3: Wh/o?
                                       S2: You know. Professor Bhutto.

car insurance doubled / what

got a ticket in front of my apartment / where

should take (Kim) thirty minutes to get here / how long

the driver may go to jail / who

visit (Salim) in the hospital / where

the first thing they check is insurance / what

she'll have an operation tonight / when

5. Dialogue

Listen to the following dialogue.

Traffic Accident

Richard:	Did you see where Rosalia made the newspapers?
Salim:	What?
Richard (reading):	". . . the driver of the eastbound car, Rosalia Martinez, was thrown from the small sport convertible. Her condition is listed as 'satisfactory' at St. Catherine's Hospital."
Salim:	Let me see that. I didn't know about this.
Richard:	She's still in the hospital. I guess she looks really banged up; that's what my wife said. But she's lucky. Just one broken rib and a concussion.
Salim:	What happened?
Richard:	She was coming off the freeway onto 4th, and somebody was making a left turn, you know, illegally, and, bang! blindsided her. A DWI.*

_____

* DWI = "driving while intoxicated."

Salim:	A who?
Richard:	A drunk.
Salim:	Did he have insurance?
Richard:	She. Nope. Of course she didn't get a scratch.

Speaking Activity

Describe briefly how the accident involving Rosalia happened, or describe an automobile accident in which you were involved.

Affixes and Stress Shift

I. Suffixes with No Stress Change

Generalization: When added to a word, some suffixes do not cause a change in stress. These suffixes include *-ness, -able, -ment, -er/or, -ly,* and *-ist.* Note that the added suffix changes the part of speech.

1. Repeat

	Noun	*Verb*	*Noun*
háppy	háppi*ness*	devélop	devélop*ment*
thórough	thórough*ness*	encóurage	encóurage*ment*
adúlt	adúlt*hood*	méasure	méasure*ment*
néighbor	néighbor*hood*	repláce	repláce*ment*
cráftsman	cráftsman*ship*	atténd	atténd*ance*
fríend	fríend*ship*	insúre	insúr*ance*
óperate	ópera*tor*	propóse	propós*al*
démonstrate	démonstra*tor*	appróve	appróv*al*
týpe	týp*ist*	fárm	fárm*er*
biólogy	biólog*ist*	wórk	wórk*er*
rápid (adj.)	rápid*ly* (adv.)		
prófit (n.)	prófit*able* (adj.)		
wónder (n.)	wónder*ful* (adj.)		
béauty (n.)	béauti*ful* (adj.)		

2.   Practice

When you hear the teacher say a word from the previous list, respond with the corresponding word of the pair.

Examples:

T:		*S:*	
	háppy		háppiness
	fárm		fármer
	adúlthood		adúlt
	biólogy		biólogist
	insúrance		insúre
	rápid		
	propósal		
	etc.		

II.   Suffixes with Stress Change

Generalization: When suffixes like *-ity, -ar/al, -cal,* and *-tion* are added to words, stress may move toward the end of the words. Note the change from one part of speech to another when the suffix is added.

1.   Repeat

Adjective	*Noun*	*Verb*	*Noun*
stúpid	stupídity	génerate	generátion
respónsible	responsibílity	líberate	liberátion
áctive	actívity	imágine	imaginátion
cápable	capabílity	démonstrate	demonstrátion
sénsitive	sensitívity	éducate	educátion
sénsible	sensibílity	óperate	operátion
rélative	relatívity	órganize	organizátion

Noun	*Adjective*
hístory	histórical
biólogy	biológical
geólogy	geológical
áccident	accidéntal
expériment	experiméntal
fámily	famíliar

2.   Practice

When you hear the teacher say a word from the previous list, respond with the contrasting form.

Examples:

T: stúpid	S: stupídity
génerate	generátion
geológical	geólogy
operátion	óperate
fámily	
sensitívity	
etc.	

III. Stress

1.   Repeat

proféssional training	acadêmic background
góvernment íntern	management trainée
láboratory researcher	applicátion process
biológical sciences	príor appróval

Your applicátion hasn't been appróved yet.
Your emplóyer will spónsor the applicátion.
An ínternship is part of your educátion.
It's a pósition in the résearch and devélopment department.

2.   Identify

Listen to the following sentences and mark the stressed syllables.

Example: You háve to submít this requést to ÍŃŚ.

1.   Economic growth has slowed down.

2.   The government is tightening up its requirements.

3.   Some applications are closed to non-citizens.

4.   Your prospective employer has to be committed to hiring you.

5.   You'll need recommendations from your professors.

3. Change the Phrase

Change the verb phrase to a noun phrase with *of*.

Examples:

Verb Phrase	*Noun Phrase*
investigate the problem	the investigation of the problem
replace the old system	the replacement of the old system
examine the data	the examination of the data
develop your economy	
re-organize the government	
submit the report	
propose an idea	
solve the problem	
demonstrate the solution	
measure the results	
complete the application	
approve the application	

4. Practice

Answer the questions using a different form of the underlined word.

Examples:

T: Have you had an <u>internship</u> before?

S: Yes, I was an intern at the local newspaper last summer.

T: What were your <u>responsibilities</u>?

S: I was responsible for part of the advertising campaign.

T: What do you <u>imagine</u> yourself doing five years from now?

S: In my imagination, I see myself editing a newspaper back home.

Are you interested in an <u>internship</u> in marine biology?
Have you applied for any professional <u>trainee</u> positions?
Did you ever work as a <u>management</u> trainee?
Are you good at finding <u>solutions</u> to technical problems?
Did you work as an <u>educator</u> before?
How are your <u>organization</u> skills?
What experience did you have that helped you develop your <u>sensitivity</u> to people of different backgrounds?
Did your university experience include laboratory <u>research</u>?
Do you think that a career in <u>medicine</u> should be profitable?
Would you encourage young people in your country to go into <u>law</u>?

5. Prepare a Speech

Prepare a one-to-two-minute description of the job you think you are (or will be) best qualified to do. Explain why you feel you are qualified.

You may want to use some of the following terms:

academic background	professional experience
employment history	on-the-job training
preparation	qualification
government job	private industry
management	trainee
internship	researcher
education	volunteer work

Clusters with /s/ and /z/

I. Recognition

1. Repeat

sleep	Spain	stick	small	strike	spring
slight	speed	stay	smoke	stress	spread
slip	speak	square	snack	string	scratch
slow	spend	squeak	sweep	straw	scream
slap	spoon	squall	swat	strange	scrape

laughs	rats	lacks	priced	lists
chiefs	cheats	drinks	east	costs
lamps	hunts	links	cost	tastes
hips	prince	strikes	taste	wastes

2. Repeat

ribs	leads	legs	arms	lens	cars
labs	rides	tags	limbs	runs	doctors
tabs	lids	rugs	rooms	physicians	drivers

leaves	lends	surprised
gloves	wounds	amazed

II. Stress

1. Repeat

a stáy in the hóspital

emérgency room physícians

inténsive cáre unit

admíssions desk

résidents and ínterns

sémi-private rooms

the pharmacéuticals industry

diagnóstic tests

She's álways been scáred of hóspitals.
They're wáiting for the resúlts of tésts.
She'll háve to rést at hóme áfter she's reléased.
Ínsurance will cover párt of the costs.

2. Read and Look Up

1. He reduced his speed when he saw a police car.
2. Both drivers were injured in the accident.
3. Her name wasn't on the hospital's list of patients.
4. We stopped to ask at the admissions desk.
5. It would cost thousands of dollars to repair the car.
6. She was also concerned about the high costs of hospitalization.
7. We expect she'll be released from the hospital soon.
8. The doctor's recommendations are to stay home and rest for a few days.

III. Intonation

1. Review of Patterns

Repeat.

1. You have a valid driver's license, don't ⁄you?
2. What do you remember about the ac\cident?
3. How long do you have to stay in the ho\spital?
4. You forgot to bring my books, did\n't you?
5. Can't I sign my own release f⁄orm?
6. You're going to say I should stay here longer, r⁄ight?
7. If it's just headaches and broken ribs I can take pain pills, you kn⁄ow?
8. It was worse than a little fender bender, but I'm OK, O⁄K?

2. Dialogue

Listen to the following dialogue. Mark the intonation lines on question tags.

Rosalia Leaves the Hospital

Harriet: You have relatives in this country, don't you?

Rosalia: My aunt. But don't call just yet, OK? It's her car that's all smashed up.

Ramon: We brought you something you really like, you know?

Rosalia: Chocs?

Harriet: Textbooks.

Rosalia: You guys are not too bad, are you? Now just give me a ride home, and I'll be happy.

Harriet: Whoa, what do the doctors say?

Rosalia: You know doctors, right? They worry. A hundred more tests and two years in inten-

sive care. That's what they say.

Ramon: Maybe you should just rest another day or two, huh?

Rosalia: Maybe you should take my final exams for me, huh? No, thanks. I'll sign my own

release papers if I have to.

3. Practice

Work with a partner. Get some information about your classmate's experience in a hospital. Then briefly explain to the class what you have learned.

Here are some sample questions you might ask.

> When did you have to go to the hospital?
> How did you get there? Ambulance?
> Why did you have to go in?
> Did they have to operate on you?
> Was it scary?
> How long were you there?
> Did insurance cover the costs?
> Can you describe the room you were in?
> What was the best part about the experience?

Affixation and Vowel Change

I. Vowel Change

Generalization: Vowels may change when some words appear in different forms.

Examples:

v**ai**n	v**a**nity
ass**u**me	ass**u**mption
w**i**de	w**i**dth

1. Repeat

/e/	/æ/		/(y)u/	/ə/
v**ai**n	v**a**nity		ass**u**me	ass**u**mption
n**a**tion	n**a**tional		res**u**me	res**u**mption
n**a**ture	n**a**tural		red**u**ce	red**u**ction
gr**a**ve	gr**a**vity		pres**u**me	pres**u**mption
s**a**ne	s**a**nity		prod**u**ce	prod**u**ction
gr**a**teful	gr**a**titude		cons**u**me	cons**u**mption

2. Practice

When you hear one form of the word from the above list, respond with the other form of that word.

Examples:

T:	vain	*S:*	vanity
	natural		nature

3. Repeat

/i/	/ɛ/		/o/	/a/
br**ie**f	br**e**vity		comp**o**se	comp**o**site
d**ee**p	d**e**pth		ph**o**ne	ph**o**nic
rev**ea**l	rev**e**lation		p**o**se	p**o**sture
pr**e**side	pr**e**sident		imp**o**se	imp**o**ster
pr**e**cede	pr**e**cedent		ev**o**ke	ev**o**cation

112

app*ea*l   app*e*late   prov*o*ke   prov*o*cative
pr*e*vail   pr*e*valent

4. Practice

When you hear one form of a word from the above list, respond with the other form of the same word.

Examples:

T: brevity   *S:* brief
    compose   composite

5. Repeat

/ay/   /ɪ/

w*i*de   w*i*dth
w*i*se   w*i*sdom
div*i*de   div*i*sion
inv*i*te   inv*i*tation
reconc*i*le   reconc*i*liation
insp*i*re   insp*i*ration
real*i*ze   real*i*zation
telev*i*se   telev*i*sion

6. Practice

When you hear one form of a word from the above list, respond with the other form of the same word.

Examples:

T: wide   *S:* width
    television   televise

II. Stress

1. Repeat

withóut précedent   presúmed ínnocent
máss prodúction   consúmer príce index
télephone cónferencing   divísion of lábor
preváiling opínion   redúction in fórce

Thís prógram is télevised líve.
I hád to túrn dówn the invitátion.
We assúmed the exám would be "ópen bóok."
I have an exám I'm suppósed to prepáre for.

2.   Read and Look Up

1. I only have a day to prepare for this econ test.
2. I'm grateful for the invitation, but I don't have time.
3. I didn't realize there would be a written and an oral exam.
4. A real research paper is not like a composition.
5. You can't improvise an assignment like that.
6. I suppose I could ask the professor for an incomplete.
7. They don't realize what kind of course load I've got this semester.
8. I don't get inspired by socializing.

3.   Change the Form

Make a noun phrase.

Examples:

T: produce goods   *S:* the production of goods
        revise a composition   the revision of a composition

divide profits
reduce debt
provoke an argument
reconcile friends
compose music
presume innocence
assume debt
reveal facts
consume food

III. Intonation

1.   Review

Repeat.

1. She's just out of the hospital, r/ight?
2. Is she going to do her final ex/ams?
3. She could have just stayed in the hospital, could\n't she?
4. I mean, what excuse have we\ got?
5. This exam is really important, you kn/ow?
6. I've got to use this preparation time, O/K?

2.   Paraphrase the Sentence

Say the sentence in another way.

Example:

T: Gratitude is rare.   *S:* People aren't usually very grateful.
     Vanity is not.   People are often vain.

His assumptions are false.
There's always a presumption of innocence.
Industrial production is down.
Consumption of imported goods has gone up.
Brevity is the soul of wit.
The case went to appellate court.
The debate was televised.
It lacked spontaneity.

3.   Dialogue

Listen to the following dialogue. Mark the stress of the underlined words.

Invitation to a Baseball Game

Salim: No, no, econ test the next morning.
Kim: It's not like it will take all evening. Just a couple of hours. How long can a ball game
            last?
Salim: Too long. It cuts into my preparation time.
Kim: And it's the last time we'll get together as a group.
Salim: I know, I've gone to all the other stuff, the international dinner, the international talent
            show, the international art exhibition, the international picnic, the international new year's
            party — all that stuff. But I have to study for this test.
Kim: Oh, come on. It's just a test.
Salim: This is economics. This is not like English, this is for real. I mean, that's what I'm
            supposed to be here for. Not to go to ball games.
Kim: Sure, but what's the good of traveling to another country if you just study all the time?
Salim: This is what I do. This is what my government sent me here for.
Kim: OK, Salim, but we'll miss you.

Fill in the blanks of the admission ticket to a baseball game. Briefly describe the ticket information to your classmates.

473-800924   Aroma Dome
Admit 1   I-5/Exit 274

Aroma Dome Events, Inc.
PRESENTS

Great Falls _____   Section:_____

vs.   Row:_____

                                         Seat #:_____

Coral Gables_____

Date: M _____   D _____   Yr_____

Game Time: _____ P.M.

Suffixes and Stress Change; Falling Intonation in Yes/No Questions

I. Suffixes

Generalization: When some endings, such as *-ic*, *-(a)tion*, and *-ial* are added to words, stress shifts toward the end of the word. The vowel of the new stressed syllable may be changed. Note that the part of speech changes when the suffix is added.

Examples:

sýllable	syllábic
éditor	editórial
exámine	examinátion

---

1. Repeat

Verb	Noun	Noun	Adjective
édit	edítion	pólitics	polítical
exámine	examinátion	depártment	departméntal
órganize	organizátion	philósophy	philosóphical
prepáre	preparátion	éditor	editórial
antícipate	anticipátion	scíence	scientífic
expéct	expectátion	réal	realístic
partícipate	participátion	sýllable	syllábic
applý	applicátion	geólogy	geológical

2. Practice

When you hear the verb form, say the noun form. Or, if you hear the noun form, say the verb form.

Examples:

T: édit	*S:* edítion
organizátion	órganize

edit	examination
expect	apply
preparation	

117

3.   Practice

When you hear the noun, say the adjective. If you hear the adjective, say the noun.

Examples:

T: scíence   *S:* scientífic
      polítical   pólitics

politics
editor
philosophy
syllabic
science

II.   Stress

1.   Repeat

departméntal requírements   editórial policy
an óral examinátion   realístic expectátions
stúdent participátion   a consérvative éstimate
a prepáred spéech   polítical scíence

The óld admíssions policy is únder revíew.
I thínk the depártment will be reórganized.
My applicátion is únder considerátion.

2.   Read and Look Up

1. She felt that her academic preparation was adequate.
2. The admissions office requested a telephone interview.
3. The seminar course requires a lot of student participation.
4. I don't agree with their editorial philosophy.
5. It's not realistic to expect to get accepted everywhere.
6. If I can prepare myself, I usually do well in oral examinations.
7. The department said my transcripts didn't arrive on time.
8. I have to organize my thoughts before I call the admissions office.

III. Falling Intonation

Generalization: Sometimes falling intonation occurs with Yes/No questions. This may happen if someone asks a series of questions at one time, as in an interview. Yes/No questions with falling intonation are ordinarily not as polite as those with rising intonation.

1.   **Repeat**

    1. Are your grades \OK?
    2. Have you ever had a scho\larship?
    3. Did you fill out the scholarship \form?
    4. Are your references \complete?
    5. Did you ever apply befo\re?
    6. Are your transcripts \on file?
    7. Have you paid your applica\tion fee?
    8. Did you do the inter\view?

2.   **Practice**

Select one person to be an applicant to graduate school. Go through a checklist of questions (as in part III, section 1 above) to find out if the application is complete.

    Examples:

    Did you take the GRE?
    Did you ask for financial aid?
    Have you written the "statement of purpose"?
    Did you get the application in the mail on time?

3.   **Dialogue**

Listen to the following dialogue. Find two other forms of each of the underlined words. Use a dictionary if necessary.

               After the Grad School Interview

    Salim: So, what's the verdict?
    Rosalia: Don't know. They <u>deliberate</u> a while. I'll be <u>notified</u> by mail.
    Salim: Do you feel like it went OK?
    Rosalia: I was <u>prepared</u>. And it was what I <u>expected</u>, I guess.
    Salim: You don't seem too happy about it.
    Rosalia: I don't know if I want to go to grad school here. The department is kind of <u>divided</u>, you know what I mean. A lot of <u>politics.</u>
    Salim: So, what's new?
    Rosalia: They're okay, I guess. A couple of them are real <u>active</u>, <u>professionally</u>. Kind of <u>traditional</u>, though.
    Salim: Well, are you going to accept if they <u>admit</u> you?
    Rosalia: Depends on <u>financial</u> aid.

Word Forms

Be prepared to say them aloud.

1. deliberate _____ _____

2. notified _____ _____

3. prepared _____ _____

4. expected _____ _____

5. divided _____ _____

6. politics _____ _____

7. active _____ _____

8. professionally _____ _____

9. traditional _____ _____

10. admit _____ _____

11. financial _____ _____

Affixation and Consonant Change

I. Affixes and Consonants

Generalization: When a suffix is added to some words, a consonant in the word may undergo a change.

Example: /d/ changes to /dʒ/

resi*d*ue	resi*d*ual
gra*d*e	gra*d*ual
mo*d*e	mo*d*ular

Note that vowel change and stress shift may occur. In this example the part of speech has also changed—from noun to adjective.

1.   Repeat

Noun /d/	Adjective /dʒ/	Noun /t/	Adjective /tʃ/
grade	gradual	fact	factual
residue	residual	right	righteous
mode	modular	resident	residential
		president	presidential

2.   Repeat

Note that a silent letter may become sounded.

Noun	Adjective
muscle	mus*c*ular
column	colum*n*ist
bomb	bom*b*ard
condemn	condem*n*ation
sign	si*g*nal
resign	resi*g*nation
malign	mali*g*nant

3.   Practice

When you hear a word from the above lists, respond with the contrasting form.

Examples:

T:	muscle	*S:*	muscular
	bomb		bombard
	column		columnist

1.	fact	6.	sign
2.	right	7.	malign
3.	president	8.	modular
4.	grade	9.	damnation
5.	resignation	10.	condemn

II.   Stress

1.   Repeat

a grádual chánge	únder supervísion
fámily practítioner	an académic career
médical ínternship	eléctrical enginéering
sóftware piracy	caréer decisions

She's góing for a proféssional degree in criminólogy.
You háve to wórk for a lóng tíme únder supervísion.
I'm thínking about fámily práctice.
Befóre, he tálked abóut an académic career.

2.   Change the Form

Name the person who practices the career described.

Examples:

T:	career in medicine	*S:*	doctor (or physician)
	engineering		engineer
	plays music		musician

works with electrical wiring
a university job
career in politics
a life of crime

solves math problems
criticizes movies
coordinates publicity
supervises the work of others
works magic
does physics experiments
steals ships
explodes bombs

III. Intonation

1. Repeat

1. Why did she choose crimino‾\logy?
2. I thought he was trying for me‾d\ school.
3. Didn't she apply to grad school in C‾/anada?
4. We're all going to be rich and famous, r‾/ight?
5. I never thought he would consider engine‾e\ring.
6. How are we going to keep in tou‾\ch?

2. Paraphrase

Say the sentence in other words.

Examples:

T: Politicians have a hard life.   *S:* It's not easy to be in politics.
    She got into literary criticism.   She became a literary critic.

Physics is her field.
Ahmed's in mathematics.
His employment background included years in music.
Nearly everybody in her family has a medical career.
She works at a family practice clinic.
He does publicity for media events at the Forum.
They have civil service jobs.
She's a graduate in EE.
We'll have to get somebody to change this wiring for us.

3. Dialogue

Listen to the dialogue and do the exercise that follows.

Breaking Up

Richard:	You're done.
Kim:	Now's when it all starts, Richard. Now I get down to work.
Harriet:	You'll do fine. You'll make a really good doctor.
Kim:	I never thought I'd be going to med school.
Pawel:	So I never thought I'd go on in engineering either.
Richard:	EE's a good field.
Ramon:	I always thought we'd end up in the same MBA program. Dick, don't tell me you're switching out of business too.
Richard:	I'm going for the NBA. I'm dropping out.
Ramon:	What do you mean NBA? You never even played college ball.
Richard:	I'm trying for a walk-on.
Ramon:	This is a joke, right Harriet?
Harriet:	It better be. Dick, it's your turn to put *me* through school.

Exercise

Interview a classmate. Find out about your classmate's career and education plans. Present this information in a short talk (1–2 minutes) to the class.

Review

I. Reviewing Sounds

1. Repeat

Review the following sounds.

/ɪ/	/i/		/ɛ/	/e/
sit	seat		sell	sale
sick	seek		debt	date
still	steal		get	gate
will	we'll		test	taste
his	he's		fell	fail
it	eat		wet	wait

/ʊ/	/u/		/l/	/r/
full	fool		late	rate
pull	pool		glass	grass
should	shooed		collect	correct
could	cooed		stole	store

2. Practice

Listen to the following sentences. If the word in the blank sounds like the first word of the pair, say "one." If it has the sound of the second word, say "two."

	1	2	
1.	(it)	(eat)	There's nothing to _____ .
2.	(hit)	(heat)	I tried to _____ it.
3.	(will)	(we'll)	That _____ do for a composition.
4.	(test)	(taste)	What kind of _____ did they have?
5.	(fell)	(fail)	We'll find out if they _____ .

6.   (long)   (wrong)   She gave us the _____ one.

7.   (Collect)   (Correct)   _____ these papers please.

8.   (file)   (fire)   Don't just throw your old papers into the _____ .

9.   (glass)   (grass)   Don't walk barefoot on the _____ .

II.   Question Tags

1.   Rising Intonation

Repeat.

> *Note:*   Question tags with rising intonation are used to ask for real information.

Questions	*Answers*
You have a library card, don't/ you?	No. I haven't registered\ yet.
You talked to your advisor, didn't/ you?	Yeah. This is my new sche\dule.
The class won't meet tomorrow, will/it?	No, not on a ho\liday.
I didn't fail the test, did/ I?	No, but you didn't finish the last ques\tion.
You're going to stop at the sub, r/ight?	Yea\h. Do you want me to get you some\thing?

2.   Falling Intonation

Repeat.

> *Note:*   Question tags with falling intonation indicate that the speaker does not want new information but expects the listener to agree.

Questions	*Answers*
You forgot to edit your paper, didn't\ you?	Yes, but I'll do it la\ter.
He'll fall asleep during the exam, won't\ he?	Probably. He didn't get much sleep\ last night.
She hasn't rewritten the article yet, has\ she?	No, she says she won't do\ it.
None of them would help you, would \they?	No, they said they were too bu\sy.
You're thinking about dropping out, aren't\ you?	Yeah, but just think\ing.

3. Disagree

Note: Remember that question tags with falling intonation may seek to compel the listener to agree. If the listener disagrees, he or she may give a reason for doing so.

Examples:

T: don't have a television

    game's on now

S1: You don't have a television, $\overline{do}$\ you?
S2: Yes, I do. It's in the bedroom.
S2: The game's on now, is\n't it?
S3: No. It's tomorrow at this time.

play soccer
game's on TV
watch TV a lot
don't play baseball in (   )
didn't get tickets
forget the tickets
missed the first quarter
aren't enjoying the game

III. Emphasis and Intonation

1. Special Emphasis (Falling Intonation)

Note: When special emphasis is applied to a word in a sentence with falling intonation, the intonation falls at the point of special emphasis.

Example: I'm taking Rosalia to the clinic for her che$\overline{ck}$\up.
a. Special emphasis on *clinic*
    I'm taking Rosalia to the *cli**nic* for her checkup.
b. Special emphasis on *Rosalia*
    I'm taking *Rosali**a* to the clinic for her checkup.

Example: She has to drive her aunt's car to Den\ver.

T: aunt's
    has to

S1: She has to drive her *au**nt's* car to Denver.
S2: She *has* *to* drive her aunt's car to Denver.

1. I'm thinking about flying home next summer.

    T: home
        flying
        thinking

    S1: I'm thinking about flying *ho**me* next summer.
    S2:
    S3:

2. They planned to take a bus to Detroit.

    T: bus

         planned

         they

3. We're renting a car to go camping this summer.

    T: this

         camping

         car

         renting

4. You have to take the turnpike east for eleven miles.

    T: east

         turnpike

         have

2.   Special Emphasis (Rising Intonation)

Note: When special emphasis is applied to a word in a sentence with rising intonation, the intonation rises at the point of special emphasis.

   Example: Did your professor give you a paper to do over the holid/ays?
   a.   Special emphasis on *paper*
        Did your professor give you a p/aper to do over the holidays?
   b.   Special emphasis on *you*
        Did your professor give y/ou a paper to do over the holidays?

Example: Are you taking the biology course this sem/ester?

T: this	*S1:* Are you taking the biology course th/is semester?
biology	*S2:* Are you taking the bi/ology course this semester?
you	*S3:* Are y/ou taking the biology course this semester?

1. Are you taking the bus to Orlando this weekend?

    T: this

         Orlando

         bus

         you

2. Do you have two tickets for this Friday's concert?

    T: Friday's

         this

         tickets

         two

3. Would you like to have lunch with us at the mall Saturday afternoon?

    T: mall

         us

         lunch

4. Do you want to study in the library all weekend?

    T: all
          library
          want to

3. Double Emphasis

Examples:

T: pepper / eggs	*S1:*	Do you put p/epper in your /eggs?
	S2:	Sure, what's wrong with that?
vanilla / latte	*S2:*	Did you ask for vani/lla in your l/atte?
	S3:	Yeah, it's good that way.

ice / coffee
hot sauce / noodles
jalapeño / salad
mint / pizza sauce
guacamole / vegetables
cinnamon / espresso
avocado / sandwich

IV. Affixation

1. No Stress or Vowel Change

Repeat.

háppy	háppiness	atténd	atténdance
adúlt	adúlthood	encóurage	encóuragement
fríend	fríendship	óperate	óperator
rápid	rápidly	prófit	prófitable

2. Stress Shift Only

Repeat.

stúpid	stupídity	bíology	biológical
imágine	imaginátion	áctive	actívity
áccident	accidéntal	éducate	educátion

3.   Vowel Change Only

Repeat.

/e/	/æ/	/u/	/ə/
vain	vanity	assume	assumption
nation	national	resume	resumption

/i/	/ɛ/	/o/	/a/
brief	brevity	phone	phonic
deep	depth	evoke	evocative

/aɪ/	/ɪ/
wise	wisdom
divide	division

4.   Consonant Change Only

Repeat.

/t/	/s/	/k/	/s/
pira*t*e	pira*c*y	medi*c*al	medi*c*ine
luna*t*ic	luna*c*y	criti*c*al	criti*c*ism
		practi*c*al	practi*c*e

/t/	/tʃ/	/d/	/ʒ/
fac*t*	fac*t*ual	explo*d*e	explo*s*ion
sugges*t*	sugges*t*ion	ero*d*e	ero*s*ion
mus*c*le	mus*c*ular		
colum*n*	colum*n*ist		

5.   Vowel Change and Stress Shift

Repeat.

rev*éa*l	rev*e*látion	hóst*i*le	host*í*lity
sýmpath*y*	sympath*é*tic	réal*i*ze	real*i*zátion

6.   Stress Shift and Consonant Change

Repeat.

médi<u>c</u>al	medí<u>c</u>inal
póliti<u>c</u>s	polití<u>c</u>ian
públi<u>c</u>	publí<u>c</u>ity
músi<u>c</u>	musí<u>c</u>ian

7.   Paraphrase

Say the sentence in different words.

Examples:

T: Attendance is compulsory.   *S1:*   You have to attend.
      I'd love to be able to earn a living playing music.   *S2:*   I'd like to be a musician.

Her bad grades aren't due to stupidity.
Software piracy is a common problem in academia.
He didn't get much encouragement to go on to grad school.
Critical comments won't win you many friends.
She got no end of suggestions and advice from her friends about how to get financial aid.
There was an atmosphere of hostility in the room.
They have a law practice in another state.

V.   Intonation

1.   Question Words

Practice.

> *Note:*   The ordinary falling intonation on question words indicates that the speaker is requesting information. A rising intonation indicates surprise or a desire for repetition and further explanation.

Examples:
T: where / go on vacation (Antarctica)   *S1:*   Guess where I'm going on vacation?
                                              S2:   Where?
                                              S1:   Antarctica.
                                              S2:   Where?
                                              S1:   It's a geology expedition.

T: what / having for dinner (Ethiopian food)

S2: Guess what we're having for dinner?
S3: What?
S2: Ethiopian food.
S3: What?
S2: Yes. Salleh's cooking it.

where / have lunch (the White House)
who / coming to our class (Dean of Students)
when / going back home (this weekend)
how / I did on the test (94th percentile)
what / got for my birthday (a plane ticket)
who / going to be on TV today (me)
where / I'm going to school next year (Quebec)